Architecture
after Covid

Architecture after Covid

ALBENA YANEVA

BLOOMSBURY VISUAL ARTS
LONDON • NEW YORK • OXFORD • NEW DELHI • SYDNEY

BLOOMSBURY VISUAL ARTS
Bloomsbury Publishing Plc
50 Bedford Square, London, WC1B 3DP, UK
1385 Broadway, New York, NY 10018, USA
29 Earlsfort Terrace, Dublin 2, Ireland

BLOOMSBURY, BLOOMSBURY VISUAL ARTS and the Diana logo
are trademarks of Bloomsbury Publishing Plc

First published in Great Britain 2023

Copyright © Albena Yaneva, 2023

Albena Yaneva has asserted her right under the Copyright, Designs and Patents Act, 1988, to be identified as Author of this work.

For legal purposes the Acknowledgements on p. xi constitute an extension of this copyright page.

Cover design: Eleanor Rose
Cover image @ Laboratorio Permanente

All rights reserved. No part of this publication may be reproduced or transmitted in any form or by any means, electronic or mechanical, including photocopying, recording, or any information storage or retrieval system, without prior permission in writing from the publishers.

Bloomsbury Publishing Plc does not have any control over, or responsibility for, any third-party websites referred to or in this book. All internet addresses given in this book were correct at the time of going to press. The author and publisher regret any inconvenience caused if addresses have changed or sites have ceased to exist, but can accept no responsibility for any such changes.

A catalogue record for this book is available from the British Library.

A catalog record for this book is available from the Library of Congress.

ISBN: HB: 978-1-3502-7107-4
PB: 978-1-3502-7106-7
ePDF: 978-1-3502-7108-1
eBook: 978-1-3502-7109-8

Typeset by Deanta Global Publishing Services, Chennai, India
Printed and bound in India

To find out more about our authors and books visit www.bloomsbury.com and sign up for our newsletters.

For Alessandro Armando and Giovanni Durbiano

CONTENTS

Figures ix
Acknowledgements xi

Introduction: The return of Dr Rieux 1
  Responses to the pandemic 5
  'Distant' as a new form of knowledge 7
  Architecture after Covid-19 10

1 A 'parasite' in the city 19
  Occupying space 19
  Architecture and illness 22
  Virus, lab, city 26
  The laboratorization of space 32

2 The laboratorization of urban space 37
  Deserted cities, empty buildings 40
  Counting bodies 44
  Spacing, distancing 50
  Contactless lives 56
  Sanitizing, face covering 60
  The new 'modulor' 64
  Pandemic pictograms 67
  De-centring the disease 70
  The power of entrapment 75
  Urban metamorphosis: The new technologies of containment and visibility 77

3 Pandemic variations of design practice 81

Routines: The 'magic' of the office space 86
Slowing down: The return to the verbal, the written and the sketch 102
Stepping aside and speeding up: Technological developments 121
New compositions: Reconnecting with the 'others' 131
Innovation in practice 144

Conclusion: Architectural research extended to things 147

Historicity and virus 150
New reflexivity, new methods 152

Notes 157
Bibliography 162
Index 172

FIGURES

I.1 Sematic map of the architectural debate 8
1.1 'Diffusion model' and 'Translation model' 31
2.1 Deserted Turin – Piazza San Carlo, April 2020 40
2.2 The London tube in August 2020 41
2.3 Traffic lights system at the entrance of stores, November 2021 45
2.4 Signage in the elevator, August 2020 46
2.5 Temperature checkpoint at a shopping mall in Shanghai, November 2021 47
2.6 Temperature-measuring camera at an events venue in London, November 2021 49
2.7a Social-distancing poster, Manchester, July 2020 51
2.7b Social-distancing floor signs, Marseille, July 2020 51
2.8a Airport bus in Marseille, France, July 2020 52
2.8b Seating arrangement in bus, July 2020 52
2.9a Floor signage indicating one-way circulation system, August 2020 53
2.9b Floor signage indicating one-way circulation system, May 2020 53
2.10 Perspex partitions in restaurants, August 2020 55
2.11 QR code for contactless shopping at a store in Buenos Aires, Argentina, February 2021 58
2.12 Mask vending machine in a shopping mall in Shanghai, China, November 2021 60
2.13a Hand sanitizer at Nice airport, France, July 2020 61
2.13b Small hand sanitizers at Piccadilly station, Manchester, July 2020 61

2.14	Documents sanitizing machine, Schiphol airport, Amsterdam, the Netherlands, September 2021	63
2.15	Series of pictograms showing the sequence of operations for hand washing, Dubai airport, November 2021	65
2.16	A poster with pandemic pictograms in stores, UK, September 2020	69
2.17	A church turned into a vaccination centre, Didsbury, Manchester, December 2021	73
3.1	Architects from Hassell Studio in London discussing around a wall	87
3.2	The offices of Kevin Daly architects, Los Angeles	93
3.3	Rena Sakellaridou from RS SPARCH in her office in Athens	100
3.4	Zoom brainstorming of the team of arquiteto paisagista in Rio de Janeiro	104
3.5	Hand sketching at Mark Gage architects	116
3.6a	Group meeting of architects from Athfield Architects via screensharing during the pandemic	117
3.6b	Group meeting of architects from Athfield Architects in Wellington before the pandemic	118
3.7	Face-to-face meeting with clients in the office at Shing & Partners Design Group in Guangzhou, China	123
3.8	Work at the firm 'Seven Architecture', Manchester, UK	130
3.9	Meeting with communities and the architect's surrogate at Fake Industries	135
3.10	Hybrid meeting of the team of Brenne Architects at the Orangery Palace	137
3.11a	Hybrid meeting of the architects from l'atelier d'architecture autogérée with communities at Agrocité Bagneux, March 2021	139
3.11b	Agrocité Bagneux, March 2021	140

ACKNOWLEDGEMENTS

The idea about this book emerged during the global pandemic, in Spring 2020, in lockdown, and gradually crystallized during many long walks with my family in green Cheshire and over different international travels. I was incredibly lucky to have amazing groups of students from the United Kingdom, Argentina, Germany, Canada, the United States and China, and to experiment, think and test with them some of the ideas on pandemic cities across different contexts from Manchester to Buenos Aires, from Berlin to New York, from Montréal to Beijing. Many colleagues helped me contact architectural practices around the world: Alessandro Armando, Ipek Türeli, Reto Geiser, Gabriel Hernandez, Dorit Aviv, Sophia Psarra, Charles Rice, Peter Connely, Shreya Kochatta, Ahlam Sharif, Gareth Doherty, Vincent Duvallon, Athina Moustaka, Ola Uduku, Laurent Stadler, Julian Varas, Rob Hyde, Sabine Hansmann, Demetra Kourri, Ted Cavanagh, Jen-Pierre Chupin, Mari Lending, Lidia Gasperoni, Edoardo Bruno, Michele Bonino, Ognen Marina among others. I am greatly indebted to them.

For feedback at different stages of this project I would like to thank Bruno Latour, Beatriz Colomina, Dana Cuff, Alessandro Armando, Brett Mommersteeg, Regina Bittner, Aaron Richmond, Ipek Türeli, Lidia Gasperoni, Jörg Gleiter, Mattias Böttger, Klaus Platzgummer, Christophe Barlieb and four anonymous reviewers. Discussions with colleagues and doctoral students at McGill University (annual lecture in Spring 2021), the Bauhaus academy, TU Delf, Copenhagen University, TU Berlin, Universidad Torcuato Di Tella, and the Deutsches Archiektur Zentrum, among others, provided opportunities to discuss some of the arguments and the methodology of the book. My students, Demetra Kourri, Ramiro Piana, Chao Wang, Alexandra Arènes, Fadi Shayya, Antonella Pataro and Daniela Freiberg, helped with the illustrations while Ben Blackwell provided unique support with the semantic mapping of the architectural media discourse. James Thompson and Alexander

Highfield from Bloomsbury Publishing offered precious editorial advice and support. My family – Martin, Christian and Svet – was amazingly patient, loving and supportive, as ever. The work of my academic friends, Alessandro Armando and Giovanni Durbiano, provided a great source of inspiration. This book is for them.

Introduction

The return of Dr Rieux

In February 2020 – what feels like 'another time' now – I found myself swept away by one of my favourite books from high school, *La Peste* by Albert Camus. Page after page, the distant and enigmatic Mediterranean walled city of Oran depicted by Camus grows closer to us – the pirouettes of the only inhabitant of the deserted streets, the wind; black human figures on the empty square; piles of dead rats; Dr Rieux visiting a patient's house; the city fading away behind the shades of dust and boredom; the humidity and thick silence; the lost 'copper' glamour of the happy seasons. Then, the plague city of Oran becomes reminiscent of the city of Wuhan and, gradually, of the many other cities around the world to which the Covid-19 virus has spread, setting the stage for new kinds of existentialist dramas. As the pandemic spread, walls of different sorts were raised around cities, regions and countries as an invisible nonhuman killer marched confidently through these spaces causing major spatial transformations at different scales.

The media storm over the past months has led us to believe that the virus somehow managed to escape the conditions of its occurrence. As if it could travel on its own from distant Wuhan. Yet, an isolated virus is a pragmatic absurdity! A virus cannot survive without humans, shared spaces and transmission techniques that are necessary to activate it and keep it in existence. Equally, it cannot be detected (or stopped) without the know-how, the instruments, the resources, the expertise and the laboratory settings needed to identify it. In other words, it always remains tied to a circumscribed and well-defined spatiotemporal set of relations. As the pandemic exacerbated and politicized existing social issues, amidst the fear of a global recession and various conspiracy theories, we have been reminded to take seriously the local, material and spatial settings that accompany viruses throughout their lives. As the crisis unfolded, health measures and protocols aimed at mitigating the spread of the virus were introduced in cities across the world, transforming their profile utterly, turning them into *pandemic cities*.

With bewilderment and angst, we witnessed an unprecedented *laboratorization of urban space*: purpose-built spatial settings reminiscent of laboratories and wards have been erected on campuses, car parks, airports and train stations. Introducing lab elements and gestures into standard typologies, the virus has transformed all kinds of public space and amenity into *dispositifs* of capture: as the virus is captured, it is capturing us and thus gradually modifying the conditions of urban life. The pandemic *dispositif*, a concept inspired by Michel Foucault (1980) and Gilles Deleuze (1992), is understood here as a physical mechanism and a heterogeneous ensemble consisting of architectural forms, spatial instructions, administrative measures, discourses, technologies and institutions, which enhances and maintains the exercise of power within a pandemic society. It is a network of relations that can be established between these elements. As such, it is not an enclosed space, but a skein, a multilinear setting composed of lines of different natures – lines of visibility, articulable or implicit utterances, positioning bodies and objects, following directions and tracing processes that are always out of balance. In brief, these are spatial machines that make city dwellers see, talk, avoid touch, position their bodies and relate to each other differently. Consequently, through these *dispositifs*, a new spatial choreography of daily life has unfolded: as we followed arrows in a supermarket or complied with the varied 'distancing' requirements to talk to our neighbours, we became part of the Covid-19 spatial network too. Tested as the carriers of the virus, urban dwellers have all become subjects and participants in these experiments, part of its conditions of existence. 'Urban dwellers' are, however, not to be understood here as a homogenous group – some people fled to the mountains, others stayed in the cities, those who stayed did not always abide by the rules. In addition, the institutions, the guidelines, and the regulations varied from one state to another, from small villages to big cities, from central neighbourhoods to suburbs.

Spread all over the urban spaces, and taking different shapes, the specially devised lab-like settings have changed existing spatial conventions in cities and architectural typologies. The intrusion of this new agent into cities had triggered new material, spatial and technological inventions, new energy and most importantly, a new balance in the reordering of urban things. It also instigated a redefinition of the social relations through which cities had previously held together. As we witnessed the invisible troublemaker invading and transforming our cities, a crowd of heterogeneous allies joined the scientists, politicians, hygienists, and began contributing to the making of urban space. This gradually forced us to rethink the social link. Just as microbes contributed to the definition of the nineteenth-century social link and pasteurism had entirely reorganized 'society' (Latour 1988), Covid-19 has contributed to the rethinking of contemporary society, to what constitutes the social today. Similarly, now, what became very visible is that society is not made by the social alone; the action of the coronavirus became part of it. As the pandemic unfolded, we witnessed literally how absurd it is to believe in the possibility to make up a society with only social connections, omitting entirely the invisible nonhumans. In fact, over the past few months, this new virus managed to reorganize society in such a different way that it moulded a new alliance between science, society and the city. It triggered a wave of changes that resulted in new technological and material urban changes. Both the myth of science done in the laboratory and powerful enough to control an unstoppable killer like the coronavirus, and the myth of a society made up of social groups, interests and laws collapsed spectacularly. Instead, the virus and the science behind it, its laboratories, became an integral part of society and transformed urban life. Moreover, the circulation of power took new forms as the events of the past year unfolded, and we have witnessed the pandemic gradually generating new sources of power, which are irreducible to those that hitherto had coded the so-called political space. Various changes also unfolded simultaneously in architectural practices. Tucked into our lockdown facsimiles of offices (basements and attics), as most of us have been, we have begun to rethink our own working habits as practitioners and the spatiotemporal envelopes of our design worlds. The pandemic gradually affected the day-to-day reality of architectural practice and set concrete challenges for designers, clients and future users. This has also triggered an awareness of the bespoke attachments of designers to other nonhumans – for example, scale models and sites. Group meetings around models or renderings, or visits to the construction site have become forgotten rituals, missed by many. Instead, architects were faced with the task of pragmatically remodelling the working 'habitat' of their practice, turning domestic spaces into workspaces, kitchen tables into drawing boards. Studios have become reminiscent of the seventeenth-century 'houses of experiments' depicted by historians of early modern science (Shapin and Shaffer 1985), where domestic and working spaces, labs and workshops coexisted under one roof, affecting both the lives of practitioners and the practical art of science. These new material settings of architectural production also led to different spatial routines and epistemic habits: new formats of teamwork, communication tactics, channels of documentary exchange, ways of 'meeting' clients or anticipating users. In brief, *the architecture of architecture* has changed as we have had to redesign both the spaces and the techniques that define us as architects. However, if it was easy to turn a dining table into a drawing board, it was not so easy to produce scale models without the right equipment, scoping instruments, materials and adhesives. Harder, even, to convince a client without their hand touching the model tucked under their nose. At the same time, the rhythm of work slowed down; no pressing deadlines, no nights spent in the office sharing a cold pizza. Some clients continued to make demands as before, while others were not as hurried because construction sites were shut. The uncertainty of the economy remained a daunting concern. The documentation grew and the tiring techniques of bureaucracy got exacerbated as more minutes, from meetings on Skype, Zoom and Google Meet, piled up. These practical adjustments in the format and rhythm of design making and the epistemic habits enticed by the new politics of space, brought more awareness to the entire material, spatial and human machinery needed to sustain the specificity of the type of practice we call 'architectural'. Just as the pandemic made us rethink law, politics and science, as Bruno Latour argued in *After Lockdown* (2021), it also prompted us, we might argue, to reconsider architecture and its vectors of action. Practitioners from all around the globe engaged in *rethinking* the ecology of their design work and found new ways of situating themselves in the world of practice.

Moreover, the mundane questions of spatiality exacerbated by the pandemic shifted scholarly attention towards a more reflexive perspective on the making, meaning and interpretation of architectural knowledge. In pedagogy, they enticed discussions on how architecture will be taught in the future, and how the interruption that the pandemic has caused will lead us to reimagine architectural education (Kulper, Crouse and Liese 2021). They also made us question how the pandemic experience will shape intellectual work, and in particular, what its effect might be on architectural scholarship (Ludewig and Leach 2020). In practise, they brought new reflexivity to the role of siting, material culture, instrumentation and spatial arrangements in architectural offices and their impact on the very nature of design. The 'pandemic formats' of practising architecture provided new opportunities to witness how architectural knowledge is marked by the specific and spatial circumstances of its making. This has inevitably furthered more reflexivity among architectural professionals on how space matters for generating spatial concepts and how different material architectures and technologies contribute to the modulation of new design ideas.

Responses to the pandemic

The Covid-19 crisis has altered the materiality of cities and deepened dramatically systemic social and geopolitical inequities, creating new territorial divides (Adams, Marenko and Traganou 2021). Responding to the pandemic, urban theorists have argued that Covid-19 has changed cities – from travel and communication to consumption and social life – so irreparably, so radically that there will never be *a return* to city life itself (Yeung, Chow and Lam 2021). Indeed, the pandemic had shuttered city centres, fostered a radical refiguration of the city, and in the process, demonstrated the importance of social links. As Peter Yeung wrote, 'Many people [had] never visited shops close to their homes before because they were busy. They didn't know their neighbours or the parks nearby. The pandemic made us discover this. We have rediscovered locality, and this has improved quality of life' (Yeung 2021). In other words, the end of the 'big' city was announced. New urban planning models were devised in the spirit of a chrono-urbanism – 'the 15-minute city' – that implies a 'new relationship between citizens and the rhythm of life in cities' (Moreno et al. 2021). Whatever the chrono-version – fifteen, seventeen or twenty minutes (Da Silva, King and Lemar 2020) – this concept aims to improve life quality by creating cities where everything residents need can be reached within minutes by foot or bike. These concepts of the city promote new versions of city life based on the idea of minimal travel between housing, offices, restaurants, parks, hospitals and cultural venues. This idea was there long before the pandemic, advocated back in 2016 with the writings of Carlos Moreno, and conceived as a response to the climate crisis, by promoting green initiatives at the neighbourhood-level, reducing travel and ever-growing urban sprawl that pushes those on the peripheries further out. Yet the global pandemic has accelerated this trend towards localization, putting the fifteen-minute city on the agenda of metropolitan areas around the world (Whittle 2020). It has placed an emphasis, in particular, on density, proximity, diversity and digitalization; these are four dimensions identified in response to the challenges that different cities across the globe have endured during the peak of the pandemic.

Other critics have engaged in generating architectural scenarios for the future, focusing, in particular, on the role of green spaces. During the period of the first lockdown, reflecting on how to transform a difficult and unexpected situation into an opportunity, the architect Stefano Boeri, for instance, was interested in how the pandemic has had the capacity to make time stop, to constitute new temporalities or rhythms, and what this has done to urban dwellers and their relations with the city. The lockdown, he argued, has helped us to appreciate the importance of green spaces and now we know that we no longer depend on city offices for our work (2021). Relaxing in the park, slowing down and not being caught in the hastiness of rushing to work have transformed the relationship between time and the city. He also suggested that villages could promote and allow for a slower form of tourism and envisaged a planet crossed by great corridors of biodiversity where forests and cities would coexist within a new balance, and where historic villages would once again become living communities. The pandemic, for Boeri, has quickened the end of 'big' cities.

Yet, as Ben Rogers, the director of the Centre for London, an urban think tank, argued in May 2020, the news of the city's death has been greatly exaggerated: 'The city is not dead yet' (Rogers

2020). In fact, he continued to argue that it might get a lot younger as more young people will be moving to cities, flocking there to build up vital social and professional networks. A number of urban theories have echoed this sentiment, disputing 'the end of cities' claims of others and advocating for the possibility that big cities will bounce back after the pandemic as they have done in the past, with a return to old norms (Overman and Nathan 2020). Nevertheless, these speculations on how the pandemic has or will have radically altered our ways of working and living in cities are still unfolding and the impact of the pandemic on architecture is still debated.

Equally, as big upheavals and political changes spawn different architectural styles that echo these new climates, we could speculate on the emergence of a new architectural style out of the pandemic political and economic debris and the crisis of capitalism (Lyon-Callo et al. 2020). As Mary McLeod (1989) had argued that the shrinking economy of the 1970s encouraged the reassessment and critique of modernism and had created the conditions for postmodernism to flourish in the booming economy of the 1980s, it remains unclear what the political and economic conditions of the pandemic will produce. Assuming that architecture is intrinsically joined to political and economic structures by virtue of its production, as its economic and utilitarian parameters make it more closely and directly connected to politics than to other arts, there might still be further speculations on the types of architectural movements and styles that could possibly flourish in connection to the economic instability instigated by Covid-19.

'Distant' as a new form of knowledge

Another possible way to make sense of this very recent past and this ongoing pandemic present is to engage in 'distant readings' of the architectural professional debate that will enable us to see broader developments and trends. Drawing on previous experiments in 'digital humanities' to map and visualize networks of relations (Yaneva 2012), a distant reading of the unfolding changes in pandemic practice provides an overview in the attempt to formulate quantitative historiography (Furet 1971; Moretti 2005). Based on digital semantic mapping (Figure I.1), this overview allows tracing

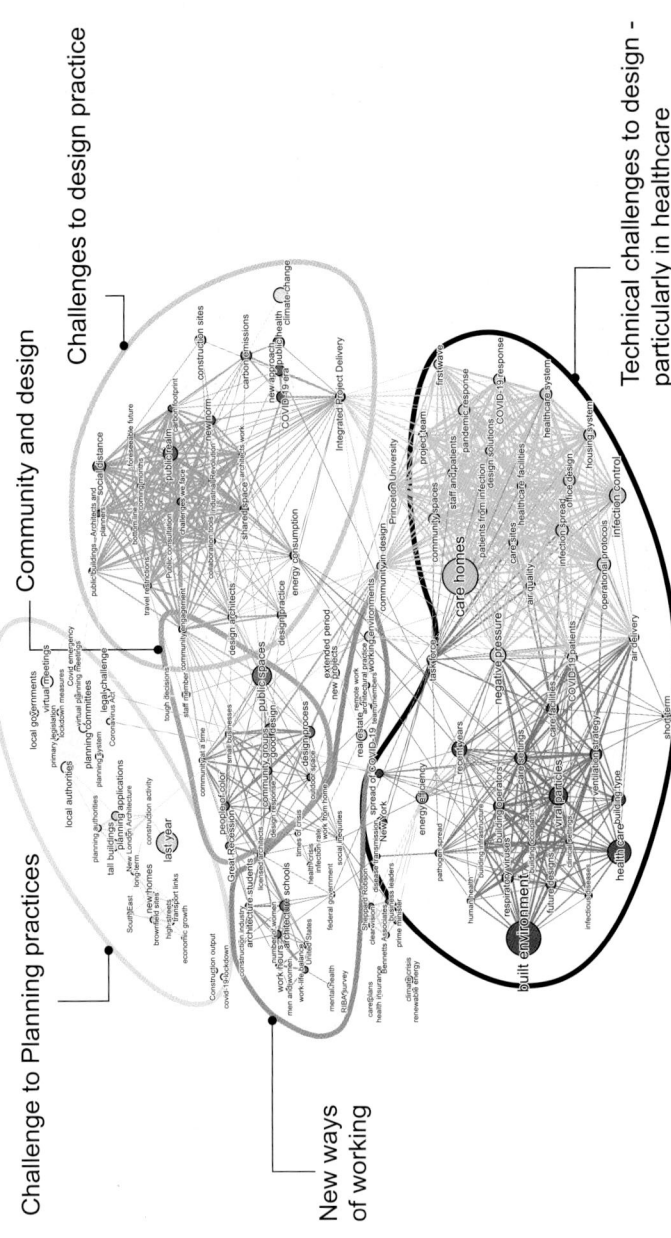

FIGURE I.1 *Sematic Map of the Architectural Debate*, © *the author and Ben Blackwell.*

some discursive patterns in the architectural debate and offers a possibility to distil key themes that emerged.

This map was produced on the basis of articles published during the pandemic in the period between March 2020 and September 2021. First, the articles were taken from the databases EBSCO and Proquest from the journals Canadian Architect, Architectural Digest, Architectural Review, Architect, Architect's journal, Architectural Record, Architectural Design, and Building Design with 'covid', 'covid-19', 'coronavirus', 'pandemic' or 'lockdown' listed as subjects. These were then narrowed down by manually reading through and removing articles with only a passing reference to Covid-19. This left a list of 255 articles. This was then put into the online software Cortext, and a list of 1,000 key terms was identified as they occurred in at least three of the documents. Through Cortext, these were then mapped as a network – in which terms appear as nodes and are connected to other terms they often appeared alongside. This network map was then put into Gephi, and spatialized using ForceAtlas 2. Smaller nodes were then filtered out to make the maps more readable and then each node was then interrogated to decide upon its relevance by cross-referencing it with its appearance in the articles. Terms that appeared a lot, but which were deemed to hold little relevance, such as 'last night', 'next month' or 'many others' were deleted in order to increase the readability of the maps. The significant clusters were then identified and interpreted by analysing the articles in which they appeared.

Looking closely and analysing this semantic map of the architectural debate we can perform a distant reading of the current situation. In distant reading, as Franco Moretti (2005) called this type of approach, distance is not an obstacle, but a specific form of knowledge. We can see fewer elements, hence a sharper sense of their overall interconnection. On a broader social level related to community and design, there is a discussion about the economic crisis related to Covid-19, and the possibility of recovery. Terms such as the 'Great recession' and 'World War' are revealing, particularly with regards to the hope that Covid-19 will spark a rebuilding effort akin to that which followed the Second World War (see the cluster on the map 'Community and design'). In a similar vein, there are references to social and environmental issues, with terms such as 'people of colour' and 'climate crisis', which reflects the way that environmental and BLM movements have intersected with the

Covid-19 crisis. While at the urban level there is a lot of reference to public and outdoor space, at the level of the practice of architecture and architectural education the focus is placed on the new ways of working with reference to 'remote working', 'work from home' and 'work life balance' and a number of issues around the impact of these ways of working from home including 'mental health', 'gender imbalance' and 'social inequalities', among others (see the cluster on the map 'New ways of working'). The specific challenges to design practice are grouped in a different cluster where we find concerns expressed around 'public consultations', 'the relations between architects and planners', 'community engagements' and 'construction sites' (see the cluster on the map 'Challenges to design practice'). On the level of planning, issues such as 'leal challenges', 'virtual planning', 'new homes' and 'planning applications' are highlighted, among others (see the cluster on the map 'Challenges to Planning practices'). On the level of particular buildings, there are discussions relating to the design of hospitals and Covid-19-safe design, as well as references to the various different building sectors, such as 'office' and 'housing' (see the cluster on the map 'Technical challenges to design'). Overall, the distant reading of the map provides an overview of the key topics and general tendencies in the architectural debate and to some extent echoes the main themes from the larger societal discussions that the global pandemic has triggered but can hardly offer insights into the concrete challenges at the level of the daily urban life or mundane design work in architectural practices.

Architecture after Covid-19

Instead of speculating on the death or rebirth of big cities, the emergence of new styles or the role of architects in a post-Covid-19 era and taking a big speculative jump into the unknown future, in this book I rather dwell on the present, slowly, meticulously, and painstakingly, in order to fully unpack and understand the range of unfolding transformations that follows in the wake of Covid-19, that is *after* Covid-19 became part of urban life. Avoiding grand manifestos and futurist rhetoric, the book keeps sights close to the challenges of design practice and downwards onto the paths of the city and as such is an attempt to theorize the present situation without historicizing it – that is, without looking backward or forward. Such an articulation is possible only in the present, a present that we live and relive, and that we re-actualize and articulate, a present that is well pronounced as it goes from one point in the present to another, not from the past to the present or the present to the future. And if the word 'future' is somewhat absent in this book, it is because, in the book, we focus extensively on a present pregnant with hesitation and on the difficulty to articulate it with clarity and determination. This difficulty to re-actualize creates the hesitations of speech, a sort of *stuttering* that is tied to hesitation, of not fully knowing *yet* what is happening or what to do. I amplify this hesitation by adding a multitude of other voices to mine – voices of media critics and urban dwellers, as well as voices of design practitioners from all over the globe, repeating and renewing these hesitations as an actualization of the present. Thus, the aim is to find a way to talk about what is difficult to express right now, think what is unthinkable and articulate what is so hard to define. In other words, to talk about what we feel and live through as we are experiencing it. However, the full articulation of these changes in the city and in architectural practice requires more distance and therefore their outright conceptualization becomes possible *with time*.

Concerned with the present, I ask: What exactly makes this enigmatic virus and the disturbances it triggers so interesting for us? Can't it be left to the scientists, the epidemiologists, the virologists and the historians of science? How does it reshape the cities we live in and the daily choreography of urban life? How does it change the practical settings and epistemic formats of architectural practice? What new reflexivity on practice does it entice? Addressing these questions, our purpose here is *not* to 'explain' the pandemic. We will not be attempting in any way to confine the analysis to factors that triggered the pandemic or to the impact and 'influences' the pandemic exerted 'on' cities or architectural practice. To do so would once again be to filter the content of architecture from its social 'environment' – a critical gesture that hampers its understanding. The only task of the analysis here is to follow and account for, slowly and meticulously, the transformations of pandemic cities and architectural practice, and all participants involved. For this reason, the presentation of the material does not follow the historical, chronological path but rather the network of associations that slowly make up the architectural world under the pandemic. By so doing, this account prompts the rethinking of the common epochal or heroic types of historiographies and offers instead an alternative approach that the pandemic has fortuitously granted.

Conceived as a long ethnographic and visual essay, this book offers a chronicle of the present, of *that* specific moment during the pandemic between the years 2020 and 2021 when the laboratory gained *the power* to invade urban space. To explore Covid-19 in the city I draw from Michel Serres (1982) and Bruno Latour (1988) to witness how the so-called 'social' actors seem to rival in ingenuity the so-called 'natural' actors in learning how to move and avoid being contaminated. First, I discuss how the omnipresence of the virus made us gradually redefine what links us all together in cities (Chapter 1). Fighting the virus together, architects, scientists and politicians all strove to make towns habitable, urban space shareable and to consolidate new networks of city planners, doctors, hygienists, virologists, biologists, public servants, policemen, engineers, security technicians, materials, technologies, signage systems and the virus, and its different variants, to ensure that we can continue to live together. An entire new choreography of collective life unfolded on the urban stage that allowed the emancipation of this unpredictable new nonhuman – the Covid-19 virus – from the double domination of society and science. Making nonhumans visible, the great upheaval of the pandemic also made us question what society is made up of, who acts and how, and who are the spokespeople for these new innumerable, invisible and dangerous nonhumans? Pandemic societies appeared as made up equally of those who bring humans together (politicians, public servants, and others) and those who bring the virus into the mix, speak on its behalf and craft different ways of controlling and isolating it (hygienists, public health experts and policemen). This made us question further the different choreographies of urban space impacted by the pandemic and the extent to which they managed to renew the political game in cities.

To account for changes in pandemic cities, I trace the laboratorization of urban space (Chapter 2) using a variety of methods: original photographs, secondary ethnographic materials (images, texts, archival materials and news reports) and 'socially distant' ethnographic observations of specific urban contexts, typologies and groups of urban dwellers from a range of cities around the world (from Manchester to Buenos Aires, from St Ives to Antibes, from Amann to Los Angeles and from Turin to Shenzhen). Witnessing how cities became deserted, roads were blocked, stadia were turned into battlefield hospitals and sports venues hosted vaccination centres, we began acknowledging the power of nonhumans and the spatial strength of their capture. Most importantly, we experienced how buildings and urban arrangements acted as *dispositifs of capture* for the virus and the humans, thus gradually modifying the conditions through which to design cities. This ethnographic material allows for depicting specific spatial metamorphoses, changes in traditional typologies and urban life, new spatial practices, new pictograms and signposting systems, and new technologies and materials. When scrutinizing urban space and buildings, I also trace sequential changes, analyse normal versus pandemic formats of functioning, and reflect on how specific material arrangements have changed and have begun facilitating news types of relations. Following meticulously what urban dwellers do – the groupings, the uses and misuses, the specific experiences – I analyse how Covid-19-related spatial arrangements facilitate or impede social groupings, and sometimes generate new forms of urban politics (Yaneva 2017).

After accounting for the spread of the lab-like settings across the city and how they act as *dispositifs* of capture for viruses and humans, I turn to analyse the small variations and minimal changes triggered by the virus in the day-to-day reality of architectural practice (Chapter 3). Drawing on an Actor-Network-Theory approach, I scrutinize how the shift to socially distanced and online forms of working due to Covid-19 restrictions has redefined the creative apparatus of practitioners. Through a range of ethnographic situations collected through the experimental format of an 'ethnographic questionnaire' with firms from forty countries, I scrutinize the new epistemic and material formats of pandemic design practice. Paying specific attention to the texture of the daily work of architects in a period of crisis, and how they adjust and appropriate space, how they refine and continue to develop their craft, can highlight the situated and embedded nature of architectural knowledge. In particular, I look at the technical innovations, the new relational dynamics between architectural firms and connected industries, the new spatial routines and epistemic habits related to design creativity, communication tactics and the new set-ups of teamwork and channels of documentary exchange. Accounting for these changes through careful 'thick descriptions' produced by practitioners from a distance reveals both the problems and the potentials that arise from these new working patterns. It offers new insights on the importance of these minimal changes for the advancement of design and sheds light on the shifting social and economic landscapes of architectural practice.

In the concluding chapter, I reflect on the way the pandemic has also made us rethink our methods of architectural research. As architectural knowledge is embodied in people and things, made through mundane and locally varying modes of social and cultural interaction, we are led to reconsider more than ever the 'social' dimension of architecture and urban design. Shadowing practitioners at work for the past twenty years – working alongside practices like OMA, FOA, Mosche Safdie and Álvaro Siza Architects, among others – I have witnessed first-hand the unique epistemic offers of ethnographic methods and their remarkable potential to investigate new research questions in architectural theory. The new conspicuousness of the 'social' that the virus has amplified forces us to ask questions about these methods and urges us to invent novel formats of enquiry that can replace and reinvent actual 'contact', immersed observation and dialogue.

The methods used in this book respond to this challenge. To analyse the changing curves of the pandemic city, a socially distant ethnography was used, relying on photographic and visual media sources to account for the shifting spatial conventions and the contactless modalities of urban life. The study with practitioners began in the Spring of 2020 during the first lockdown with a questionnaire with twenty-three Italian practices from Northern Italy – the part of Europe most affected by the pandemic at the time – followed by Zoom interviews with selected practices in the summer of 2020. This first pilot study formed the basis of an ethnographic questionnaire shared in Spring 2021 and used to conduct a socially distant ethnography and 'virtual visits' in 130 architectural practices around the world with the aim of unpacking the specific adjustments and innovations that helped them to survive during the crisis. Yet, doing distant ethnography might sound at first glance almost paradoxical as ethnography implies, by its definition, a close and immerse investigation. What I call 'distant ethnography' here points to a technique of adapting ethnography to a set of data collection tactics that could be used from a distance to account for the lived experience of designers (or dwellers), commonly accounted for in close participant observation. It is a different technique than the much-debated 'virtual ethnography' (Domínguez et al. 2007; Hine 2000), which includes various techniques for ethnographically researching social interactions that take place on the internet (newsgroups, chat rooms and web-based discussions) or 'archival ethnography', which points to a technique of adapting ethnography to a set of related documents that account for the lived experience from the past (Sahlins 1992). Like 'para-ethnography' (Holmes and Marcus 2008; Marcus 2000), distant ethnography implies a collaboration among anthropologists and research subjects; in this case – architectural practitioners with shared sensibilities to the pragmatics of design.

Many different disciplines use ethnography to approach their objects of research (such as sociology, pedagogy, philosophy, psychology or economics) and so does architecture. Incorporating ethnography as another methodological option for researching the cultural dimensions of architectural practice, the first ethnographic studies focused on architectural practitioners in an educational context (Schön 1983) and dealt with the internal life of architectural firms (Cuff 1992). Many scholars followed suit and engaged in painstaking ethnographic observations of practices around the world, which often involved years of participant observation (Farías 2015; Houdart and Minato 2009; Jacobs and Merriman 2011; Lefebvre 2018; Mommersteeg 2020; Rose, Degen and Mehuish 2014; Sharif 2016; Yaneva 2005, 2009a, b, 2018; Yarrow 2019). Yet, in Covid-19 times, the impossibility to travel and visit practices and engage in direct observation of their daily work prompted this study to adapt ethnography to a set of techniques that can be practised from a distance and bear witness to or contain explicit accounts of an everyday world of lived experience of design practitioners. Thus, 'distant ethnography' is an anthropological research technique that attempts at tracing the life of architectural practices from a distance using written records provided by the firms (project documents, presentations, reports, press clippings and other documents produced during the pandemic), distant interviews conducted via Skype, Zoom or other internet-based platforms, as well as written accounts (or ethnographic responses) by the architects and photographs supplied by them to document their experiences. This approach takes us away from the traditional Malinowskian aesthetics of intensive participant observation in communities.

During the pilot study, Zoom and Skype technologies were used to conduct interviews, 'visit' an architectural firm through a Zoom window and 'take a tour' of the office without being 'there' in person. They provided distant but useful insights into the office culture. Further, 130 firms were approached with an 'ethnographic questionnaire' and asked to describe their design routines during the pandemic. Although this was far from being a 'representative sample' of *all* architectural practices around the world, it captured a variety of ways of practising architecture in pandemic conditions. The most interesting responses came from small- and medium-scale firms. And since 76 per cent of architecture practices are of small scale, with fewer than ten people, these responses reflect the state of things in practice at the moment. Moreover, small-scale firms 'are known to be the innovators, and this has huge consequences for the built environment'.[1] Inviting these practices to engage in ethnographic reflections of their own work, to act as researchers and research objects at the same time, had challenges and difficulties. The limitations outnumbered the advantages, especially for those who have done years of real-life ethnography. First, this method challenged practitioners to actively reflect on 'what happens' in their practice, in the present tense and to articulate it; to do this they had to deliberately reduce and abstract from their practice, by choosing one particular situation to describe. Second, as the ethnographic responses focused on one particular challenge in the practice, they were limited in scope as opposed to close participant observation that can offer insights into many different simultaneously unfolding dynamics. In addition, not being able to witness these situations, the anthropologist 'observed' the practice without participating (distant ethnography thus implies distant observation) and relied solely on the architects' accounts. Overall, as designers outlined fewer elements than what an anthropologist can capture on the ground, a sharper sense of their overall interconnections was possible. This allowed tracing relations among practices from distant geographical contexts. Moreover, architects were invited to use photography in the recording of ethnographic data which offered a reflexive photographic 'way of seeing' their practices and differed from the ethnographic photography commonly used by anthropologists to document actions and events. The resulting written and visual accounts provided a selective rendering of the pandemic reality of architecture-making, and a rare peek into a world of practice that otherwise would remain opaque or invisible.

As a distinctive, and somewhat paradoxical form of ethnography, socially distant ethnography invites us to reflect on some fundamental assumptions and concepts of this method. The documents, the written accounts and images, the distant interviews and visits, are a substitute for the anthropologist's actual presence and offer a way to capture, as closely as possible, the cultural world of architectural practices. The distinctive nature of the execution of such accounts, documents and visuals allows us to imagine what happened in these practices: who was present, and where and when a designer's account was written, a document was produced or a picture was taken, just like a 'present-time', in-person ethnographer who can observe what those present say and do. Any account, visual or written, that proves valuable as a source of information on the uncertain and difficult-to-articulate present of architectural practice or the reality of the pandemic city can rightfully be considered as data for architectural anthropology.

Distant forms of commonly close methods raise important methodological questions on the relation between the researcher and the field, and the many different participants in the 'construction' of the ethnographical narrative. Although distant methods cannot fully replace the experience of close real-life ethnography, they still provide an interesting and thought-provoking way of 'being there' and generate rare insights into the complexities of architectural practice and urban life as objects of research and the many possible ways of approaching them. They also allow us to engage in a meta-reflection on the writing of disciplinary history.

CHAPTER 1

A 'parasite' in the city

Occupying space

New, small and invisible, multiplying wildly due to its smallness, producing variants, and threatening the equilibrium of cities and the vitality of entire societies: this is the *intrusion* of a new virus in 2020. It was identified initially at the end of 2019 when the World Health Organization (WHO) was informed by the Chinese government about several cases of a viral pneumonia with unfamiliar etymology. On 11 March 2020, the WHO expressed concern about the alarming levels of its spread, the severity of the disease and the level of inaction, and had declared the Covid-19 outbreak a 'global pandemic' (Cucinotta and Vanelli 2020). It called on countries to take action to contain the virus, leading, eventually, to the implementation of often severe and strict lockdown policies.

The zoonotic source of transmission of the virus to humans has not been confirmed yet; however, sequence-based analysis has suggested bats as the key reservoir or source. The International Committee on Taxonomy of Viruses (ICTV) had named the virus the Severe Acute Respiratory Syndrome Coronavirus 2 (SARS-CoV-2) and the highly transmittable and pathogenic viral infectious disease caused by it – Covid-19. Other viruses, members of the beta coronavirus group were identified in the past, for instance, the SARS-coronavirus in 2003 (SARS-CoV) and a decade later, the MERS-coronavirus, the Middle East Respiratory Syndrome Coronavirus (MERS-CoV). Both SARS-CoV and MERS-CoV are members of the beta coronavirus group and phylogenetically diverse from other human-CoV. Patients suffered from pneumonia, followed by Acute Respiratory Distress Syndrome (ARDS) and renal failure.

Yet, nothing could have prepared us for this new type of coronavirus. Scientific observations had indicated a human-to-human spreading capability, which was subsequently reported in more than 100 countries in the world. The virus has a few different transmission pathways, mainly respiratory droplet transmissions – that is, airborne transmission through close contact with an infected person, exposed to coughing, sneezing, respiratory droplets or aerosols. These aerosols can travel through the air sometimes over 6 feet and are then inhaled through the nose or mouth by any susceptible host (Shereen et al. 2020). They penetrate the human body (lungs) via inhalation through the nose or mouth. Due to the higher transmission rate, the virus spread quickly around the globe and infected millions. Millions died too – at the moment of completion of this manuscript, in February 2022, the figure of Covid-19 deaths has reached 6,195,655 million.

Due to the aerosol transmission at distance and the fact that droplets can stay in the air for up to thirty minutes, sometimes longer depending on the quality of ventilation (The Lancet Respiratory Medicine 2020), *space* became a crucial factor in the pandemic. That capacity of the virus to travel in space made it an extraordinary parasite. Here I am drawing on Michel Serres' concept of the parasite in social, biological and informational systems. Deconstructing the relationship between host and parasite, Serres suggested that the parasite is less a 'drain' on the energy of a given system, but rather something that can become a catalyst for changing its very nature. The radical implication of this idea is that the parasite is not necessarily negative – as we commonly conceptualize it – as it opens a new range of possibilities. Like any parasite the coronavirus takes hold of space by being invisible: it is 'occupying *space* with its imperceptibility' (1982: 194). Bacterium, worm, virus, bacillus, phage – seldom if ever larger than the size of an insect, have the capacity to pass, stick and intrude everywhere. And this smallness has its traps that baffle us and make us engage in activities for protecting ourselves.

It is the most silent of beings. Small, hard to catch; it cannot be felt; it keeps quiet; it listens. Yet, and this is precisely the paradox, the virus is *noisy*. It is not invisible because it hides, but by making noise. Media reports bombarded our screens with countdowns of infections, deaths, and recently vaccinations, comparisons of countries and reportages from the most affected parts of the world. No event in recent history has occupied our media attention so vividly. The noise was colossal indeed. Hiding behind the clamour, the virus sustained high noise levels for a long time. Moreover, it became invisible by being impossible. Impossible, absurd and outside logic. The capability of coronavirus to spread fluctuates and its virulence varies. Its infectious power is measured by its capability to adapt itself to one or several hosts. Thus, cities and buildings became hosts, receptacles for its parasitic action by *providing the space* for it to exist. Invading cities, uninvited, it began *parasiting* on their vitality and eating the 'bodies' of various building typologies – from the most mundane and trivial like our houses and offices to the most sophisticated, like museums and libraries. It infested and transformed them all along. Functioning like an automatic corrector, observing, troubling us all, but never troubled, it acted in an asymmetric way. There was no exchange. Gifted in some fashion, eating what is next to it, soon eating at the expense of others, always eating the same thing, the coronavirus used urban settings as flexible hosts and relied on them to continue to give, constantly, until they stretched and deformed their boundaries, until they morphed entirely, or sometimes broke.

We should note here that cities were not the prey for the virus as they offered multiple settings for controlling it. Not prey then, but *hosts*. To capture it, to take hold of it, to contain it despite its invisibility, special settings were devised across urban contexts to make it *perceptible, traceable*. Reminiscent of laboratories, these settings endorsed experimentation and examination to gain knowledge about the virus and its spread. They became instances of 'parasitic architecture' (Bollack 2013: 65) as they accounted for various architectural interventions, where small new additions cling to the original and are absorbed. They sought internal spaces between structures or attempted living on an existing structure, where they can form an opportunist beneficial use of otherwise wasted elements of the embodied structure, or sometimes the structure itself. These lab-like settings slowed down and temporarily paralysed urban life before gradually starting to reshape cities and societies. It is this concept of cities as hosts of parasitic activities, as accommodators for the multiple metamorphoses triggered by a noise-making virus with an imperceptible smallness that is crucial to unpack here.

Architecture and illness

It was not unexpected to see cities becoming the hosts of the new virus. Traditionally cities and buildings have been the accommodating hosts of viruses for they create a specific environment that facilitates the spread of disease. Residing in buildings, accommodated in, and afforded by different spatial envelopes, viruses have caused numerous diseases. Despite the long-lasting bond between architecture and illness (Forty 1980; Nickl-Weller and Nickl 2013; Schrank and Ekici 2016), the pandemic has made us question the degree to which architecture can be health-inducing or health-harming, as well as the new modalities of action of the built environment in a world of fast-spreading viruses.

How is architecture as a spatial reality related to ailments and suffering bodies? Is architecture (understood as the material effect of buildings and designed environments) capable of providing cures or alleviating pain? To what extent can it be a form of health care, of protection, or harmful to the health of the bodies that occupy buildings? Exploring the long-lasting bond between architecture and illness and taking a historical overview from Vitruvius to the Sick Building Syndrome (SBS), Beatriz Colomina (2019) argued that architecture has always relied on a specific relationship between medicine and the body. Architects have always acted as 'doctors' dissecting and slicing section cuts of the 'body' of built structures, reminiscent of surgeons who investigate the mysterious interiors of bodies to gain knowledge for better cures. In an unconventional historiographic narrative, Colomina's account unfolds around a strange main actor, not a heroic human actor – an architect, for instance – but rather a nonhuman actor, the tubercle bacillus discovered by Robert Koch in 1882. As it spread, tuberculosis led to concerns with ventilation, light, exercise and emotions. Attempting to respond to these concerns, architecture gradually became a powerful curing machine, a counter-power to the traditional house that produced the debilitating effects of tuberculosis. The new features of modern design aesthetics – roof gardens, pilotis, glass walls, clean air, natural light – became medical devices of that curing machine. While tuberculosis lurked as an ever-present threat, healthy bodies and athletic figures became the paradigmatic clients of modern architecture. Far from being a shiny functional or expressive machine, modern architecture is pictured as a cocoon for sheltering fragile and traumatized bodies. The sanatorium became the quintessential modern typology dealing with illness, with its terraces, horizontal views of the setting sun, all contributing to the machinery of the building that cures, 'a factory for the manufacturing of healthy bodies' (Colomina 2019: 91). Both the horizontality of the experience of the tuberculosis convalescent lying on the chaise and the psychoanalytic patient on the couch fighting neurotic traumas – as paradigmatic clients and occupants of modern architecture – had contributed to the medicinal effects of the sanatorium architecture and spread to other typologies to become a model for a way of life embodied in modern architecture.

Looking at more recent examples, SBS is an instance of an illness related to specific buildings whose occupants can experience symptoms such as headaches, tiredness, dryness, skin irritation and a runny nose (Burge 2004). These symptoms are caused by multiple risk factors such as air pollution, ventilation, lighting, airborne bacteria, and dust (Hosseini, Fouladi-Fard and Aali 2020). While complaints associated with occupying buildings had emerged throughout the twentieth century, it was not until 1983 that the WHO officially used the term 'sick building syndrome'. The syndrome was believed to be a main reason for workers to be absent from their jobs (Jafari et al. 2015) and by the 1990s it became one of the most investigated occupational health problems in the United States. Afflicted by headaches, rashes and immune system disorders, office workers – mostly women – had protested that their workplaces were filled with toxic hazards; yet federal investigators could detect no perceptible chemical cause (Murphy 2006). This was partly due to the challenging nature of SBS. It was different from normal illnesses as it was recognized as a constellation of symptoms, caused not by an underlying mechanism, but by the environment created by the building – the ventilation, lighting, indoor exposures to chemicals wafting from synthetic carpet, ink, adhesive and solvents.

Further research has since convincingly demonstrated that the high chance of experiencing SBS is directly related to specific building designs and the use of particular materials. A study of the Hong Kong Polytechnic University Library (Yeung et al. 1991) followed users' experiences over a period of five months. Environmental factors within the library, such as the indoor air quality, the species of common bacteria, temperature and humidity, were argued to have had an impact on the health of the library users who experienced various symptoms such as dryness and eye irritation, headaches, dizziness and runny nose. Although the symptoms were directly connected to the architectural characteristics of the building, it remains unclear which specific factors caused these symptoms. Other studies have demonstrated that the rates of ventilation have a considerable impact on the manifestation of symptoms related to SBS, and, in particular, that as the ventilation rate drops the presence of symptoms increases (Fisk, Mirer and Mendell 2009). In all cases, the specific atmosphere created inside the building due to a combination of environmental factors plays a role in accelerating the manifestation of symptoms. Therefore, it is *that* awareness that environmental health is deeply connected to building design and to the correlation between building systems and disease symptoms that guided the construction of lab-like settings in the city during the current pandemic. Fabricated quickly, they all aimed to create conditions and environments that seek to control the virus and limit its spread.

Considering the role that spatial architecture plays as a vector for the spread of viruses, numerous design innovations emerged in relation to the SARS epidemic in 2003. One of them resulted in the 'Immunised Building' built in 2007 in Hong Kong, where the transmissive respiratory disease was especially powerful (Baldwin 2006). Unlike Covid-19, however, SARS only lasted for about three months. It, nevertheless, left a significant scar on the 'social body' due to its explosive outbreak and the lack of information and resources for effective control measures (Lee 2003). As a result, a bigger awareness of public health emerged. Current Hong Kong building practices are deeply impacted by some responses to SARS. The 'SARS-immune' buildings, for instance, take measures to fight against the spread of the virus in the following ways: first, the drainage system is strictly designed to ensure there is no cross-infection; second, all rooms have a natural ventilation system in case the central air condition system requires being shut down; and third, the building can be compartmentalized into separate areas while normal operations can still undergo in the uninfected areas. Another innovation that had developed in relation to SARS, Modular Integrated Construction (MiC) is also widely used now. With its segregated design, it seeks to prevent cross-infection between units; and it stops the spread of the virus. This method is used for the temporary quarantine facilities in Hong Kong and has thus proved to be an immediate architectural 'solution' in the current global pandemic (Construction+2020).

Taking this long-standing relation between viruses and buildings into account (Brown et al. 2020), during the current pandemic several anti-virus architectural solutions have been devised to stop the virus from spreading, mitigate its impact and ensure the design of healthy urban environments (Megahed and Ghoneim 2020). As Covid-19 can be transmitted both by air and through direct and indirect contact, the potential transmission dynamics of infection related to buildings became crucial. It was established that viral particles can be directly deposited on surfaces or suspended due to natural and mechanical airflow patterns, or other sources of turbulence in the indoor environment (Cirrincione et al. 2020; Horve et al. 2020). Therefore, it became critical to rethink the microbiology of indoor spaces.

The prescribed inter-personal distance of 1.5 or 2 metres (about 6 feet) by the WHO was supposed to minimize the risk of infection. Yet, this requirement has been re-evaluated and updated many times throughout the pandemic. Recent studies have supported the hypothesis of virus transmission over 2 metres from an infected person (Setti et al. 2020) while simulations of different environmental and movement conditions have indicated that a 2 metre or 6 feet social distancing was sufficient only if the ambient air was static (Oklahoma State University 2020). These findings inevitably lead to an evaluation of the design of current buildings. For instance, after a careful study of nursery buildings with proven positive Covid-19 cases, it has been established that their architectural characteristics have an impact on the number of cases (Lovec, Premrov and Žegarac Leskovar 2020). The smaller nursery buildings that contained a smaller number of occupants facilitated the spread of the virus, due primarily to the closer contact between children and teachers. In the larger buildings, with more occupants, in contrast, positive cases were confirmed within the individual groups, but they did not appear to spread inside the building. This investigation demonstrated that the spread of the virus in indoor spaces is directly related to the architectural design of the building and connected also to the transmission pathway of the virus through the spaces. The smaller the room, the closer the occupants will be and therefore the likelihood of being in contact with an infected person's respiratory droplets in the air will increase; if there is more space within the rooms the occupants will be less likely to encounter an infected person. These studies of buildings during the pandemic made architects and urban planners rethink the architecture of indoor spaces as guided by micro-environmental factors rather than by aesthetic or technological concerns.

The awareness of how building design and spatial characteristics have an impact on the spread of the virus has triggered numerous modifications in buildings during the pandemic – some big, others small and minimal. The local spatial choreography of dwelling in buildings changed as designers tried to predict the impact of the specific environment created by buildings and the resulting microbiology of indoor spaces. Factoring more than issues of air circulation, flexible open plan designs, greenery and space for distancing, these new lab-like settings emerged in response to this acute awareness that the virus had a spatial expression and could be eventually controlled with spatial means.

Virus, lab, city

As the virus multiplied and reproduced, formed a chain and a crowd, this noisy band of things and people around it occupied more and more space. Before analysing the new urban lab-like settings facilitating these crowds and their impact on the city, let's reflect on the concept of the lab, about what happens in a lab and how it relates to society.

Several studies in the 1970s explored the relationship between science and society by arguing that it can be only understood by following scientists and engineers in their practices (Knorr-Cetina 1981; Latour 1987; Latour and Woolgar 1979; Lynch 1985, 1993; Pickering 1992). The flurry of ethnographic studies of scientific practices that has followed over the past few decades have traced the reciprocal and entangled process of tuning facts, theories, machines, human actors and social relations, and has highlighted the continual coproduction of science and society. That science cannot be spoken about without speaking about society.

More than just places where scientists work, laboratories are also places where scientific 'reality' and knowledge about it is made

(Latour and Woolgar 1979). The lab is important for scientists as it is their soldier's weapon in a battle over truth and reality – about what exists and what does not. Moreover, like the general's map of the battlefield, the lab is that special place where phenomena can be observed in a small scale, controlled and dominated. Laboratories also need money, support and patronage – a whole mobilization of social support that allows them to make claims about reality and what it consists of.

Studies of scientific practice also showed to what extent scientists rely on technologies, tools, representations and other literary artefacts. Scientists at work in labs, for instance, need instruments that provide a visual display. Instruments produce readings, which in turn, become inscriptions. An inscription is a general term that refers to all the types of transformations through which an entity is materialized into a sign, an archive, a document, a piece of paper or a trace of the process of making a fact. Inscriptions are usually two-dimensional, superimposable and combinable; they are mobile as they allow new translations of the entity in the making to happen while keeping some types of relations intact. In this sense, it is *as* inscriptions that scientific realities can travel and become part of a common experience, components of reality. As the scientific activities aiming at identifying and gaining more knowledge about the new coronavirus unfolded, the accumulation of ways of registering the manifestations of the virus and the spread of the disease increased, and the devices of inscription multiplied. These series of visual inscriptions produced by the instruments not only helped the scientists become the *spokespersons* of Covid-19 but also a part of the reality that took shape around the virus.

As spokespersons, the scientists talk on behalf of the virus, and other entities that usually are unable to talk on their own. In other words, they are able to be representatives of the natural world through the experimental setup and the inscription devices that give them the power to speak on their behalf. The strength of the spokesperson of a virus comes from the fact that she does not speak on her own, but is always *in the presence* of those represented. And scientists spoke loudly in the presence of this new coronavirus without completely knowing it. Slowly, around the virus, a larger crowd grew speaking on its behalf. In the same way that the scientists spoke on behalf of the virus, politicians too began to speak on its behalf and the citizens that they also claimed to represent.

Eventually, affected people and concerned citizen groups, networks of healthcare workers and volunteers, public health servants and others – not to mention those who contested these claims, argued that the scientists, politicians and other experts did not speak on their behalf – joined together and through them the virus sustained its noisy existence.

And yet, either in the lab or outside in 'public space', the existence of the virus is not self-evident, or something awaiting 'discovery'. In the lab, the virus is not a given thing, but emerges through its actions – it does something – which is registered by the instruments that read it and produce inscriptions. This in turn becomes the basis of scientific texts. Before it becomes a thing, an endorphin, for instance, is a readable list of performances registered with the instruments in the lab. The list of actions of that object shapes its existence; it is named after what it does and is the result of local *trials* in a lab. Thus, in their emerging state, objects are defined by trials, by experiments of various sorts in which new performances are elicited. Defining objects by *what they do* under laboratory trials, ethnographic studies of scientific practices focused on the complex and controversial nature of what it is for them to come into existence, to act and become stable actors. Similarly, the lab settings erected in public space relied on a series of operations for detecting the existence of the virus on the basis of what it can do – that is, it travels a distance, is transmitted through air droplets, causes a high temperature, a new continuous cough, a loss or change to your sense of smell or taste. This series of possible and expected performances of the virus became a mechanism for constructing those lab-like spaces in the city.

As the pandemic unfolded, the origin of the virus became a central matter of concern. Where did it come from? From which lab did it escape? What caused its emergence? The belief that the virus was just *there*, and was suddenly discovered, revealed and leaked is, however, untenable. Behind this version of the story of its origin is a particular model of scientific discovery. The idea that the virus escaped from the isolated space of a lab – a space that is purely 'scientific' – into a society (in this case, Chinese) that formed a milieu in which the virus could spread and be diffused. This 'diffusion model' (Latour 1987) was for a long time the main narrative for understanding how scientific and technological innovations spread. It, in a way, invents a society as a simple medium of different resistances through which scientific ideas travel. In consequence, we have science, on one hand, and society, on the other – both *purified* of the other – and through which one or the other has direct influence. Society determines science or vice versa, scientific discoveries determine social relations. Yet, the pandemic has made this idea of purification impossible to countenance. As the virus occupied more and more space, it became obvious that 'society' is not capable of influencing its spread on its own or speeding up 'science' in order to contain it. How can we speak of the virus without discussing how it is itself 'social'? And how could we speak of the 'science' that sought to contain it without speaking about anti-vaxxers or 'social distancing'? It was implausible to imagine a consensus among humans ignorant to the demands of that violent nonhuman, a purely social consensus that could contain it through pure will.

In the spirit of a plain diffusion model, when something goes wrong, the appeal to society or social factors is often done to seek a cause or an explanation. The Covid-19 outbreak triggered many different social interpretations that often pointed their finger at 'China'. One such explanation of the origin of the virus was that it started as a laboratory leak, caused by a laboratory-associated incident, probably involving experimentation, animal handling or sampling by the Wuhan Institute of Virology. The alternative theory shared the belief that the virus emerged from natural exposure to an animal infected with it or a close progenitor virus and pointed to the Wuhan seafood market as a place of origin. These 'wet markets' became a major talking point in the West. Yet, there is not enough evidence at that moment to support any of these theories on the origin of the pandemic to be able to fully understand the roots of the outbreak. What has remained, however, is the appeal to China and Chinese society to seek an explanation. As the variants proliferated, the tendency to blame particular countries and societies remained – variants were labelled, in the media discourse, as British, South African, Brazilian and Indian simply because they were first identified in these countries. Simple and reductive social or cultural explanations were embedded in this naming practice. Later on, the naming was changed to 'alpha', 'beta', 'delta', 'Omicron', among other variants.

Alongside these variants, the network of scientists, institutions, funding and labs grew. At the same time, as the pandemic unfolded, the Covid-19 vaccine became a top priority for scientists and governments around the world. The work in many scientific labs intensified, and the effort to battle the virus by devising the right vaccine was unprecedented. Traditionally a vaccine requires five to ten years depending on the information available about the disease and how the disease infects people and spreads. Developing a new vaccine from scratch takes considerable time and effort, which makes the Covid-19 vaccine, fabricated and implemented only a year after the outbreak, a great achievement for contemporary science. Instead of celebrating this achievement, making more noise than the virus could make, national controversies about which vaccine was quicker, more efficient or with fewer side effects broke out in the summer of 2021. Leading to anti-vaccine protests, resistance and contestation, this further slowed the progress on the vaccinations globally and subsequently slowed down the global war against the virus too.

All these events confirmed to what extent it was impossible to seek a social explanation of the spread of the virus, and how improbable it was to believe that such a social explanation will miraculously resolve the problem of its transmission. Both the concepts of 'virus' and 'society' have to be examined and deconstructed. If, instead of putting the blame on countries or labelling variants with national names, we follow the entanglements of the virus with urban space, we can witness the weaker and stronger connections that it has shaped as well as the work through which the many actors involved in controlling it were able to modify, displace and translate their various and often contradictory interests. In contrast to the 'diffusion model', this model, the 'translation model' (Figure 1.1), invites us to follow scientists, public health servants, politicians, janitors, affected groups and concerned citizens and to trace their practices, what they do to contain the virus. Listening to them, following their work, we understand that they rarely refer to social factors, Chinese society, the forces of capitalism, cultural traits and so on. In this moment of 'global confusion', they themselves do not know what their society is made of, just as scientists do not completely know everything that the virus can do and are frantically scrutinizing it in lab conditions to be able to produce the right vaccine. It is because they know about neither, and they could not rely on established definitions of the virus or the societies it spreads through, that they are so busy trying out new associations, new spatial arrangements,

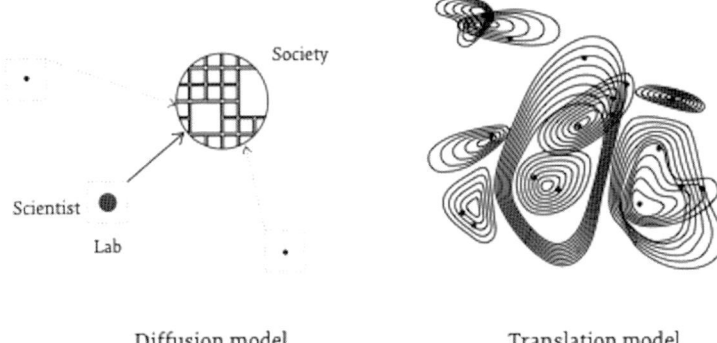

Diffusion model Translation model

FIGURE 1.1 *'Diffusion model' and 'Translation model'*, © *the author and Alexandra Arènes*

new lab-like settings to control the virus. Displacing interests, negotiating newly emerged facts, reshuffling groups, imposing new rules and recruiting new allies, this translational effort provides a more realistic reflection of the relationship between science and society, and how it has reshaped the city.

Following the lab-like urban settings will lead us to a better understanding of the pandemic, and its impact on the built environment. Equally considering the efforts to enrol and control human and nonhuman resources, these settings established a new symmetrical rapport between viruses and urban dwellers, between 'science' and various 'non-scientific' kinds of experts and actors that together reshape the city. Deployed in urban space, the lab-like arrangements connected politicians, businessmen and policemen with variants, vaccines and the technologies and materials mobilized in its prevention. All these actors moved according to different paths, reminiscent of paths on a battlefield. Accounting carefully their moves and the connections they traced, facilitated by the labs we can shed light on how these lab-like settings triggered small transformations in urban spaces and buildings, and through which viruses became part of different sets of associations, in different social relations, instead of using society as a source of explanation, and blaming the Chinese, the South Africans, the British or the Indians for producing new variants. In other words, by paying closer attention to the material networks of production through which the virus was able to travel, reproduce and vary, rather than rely on abstractions, it became impossible to maintain the division between society and science, between context and content. That is, to continue to naively believe that scientists inhabit an internal bubble cut off from the social factors on the outside; that there is a world of viruses, variants and scientists dealing with them and, at a cosmic distance, British, Chinese or South African societies. The pandemic illustrated to what extent this radical divorce between two sets of incommensurable information is a practical absurdity and its credibility doubtful.

That is why, instead of engaging in explanations, if we follow the functioning of the urban lab-like settings, we will be able to witness how scientists, hygienists, public health specialists and epidemiologists produce both the pandemic context and the things in this context. Disease and society are coproduced together. And if we are able to follow only a few actors in these lab-like settings, it is because there is a *network* that prolongs their work, an entire network of actors who contribute to the work of controlling and containing the virus. The notion of network helps to understand how so few actors manage to cover the world. The emergence of urban culture for controlling the virus is a consequence of the construction of longer networks that make us cross paths followed by others. Tracing the Covid-19 networks to see what they capture in their meshes and what escapes them, we will inevitably end up producing a relational understanding of the current pandemic transformations.

The laboratorization of space

If, for the early studies of scientific practices in the 1970s, the lab remained a tacit and neutral background of vibrant scientific activities, in the following decades, science and technology studies scholars gradually shifted their attention towards the importance of the place of experiment and the spatiality of techno-scientific practice (Forgan 1989; Gooday 1998; James 1989; Shapin and Shaffer 1985), the instrumentation and material culture of labs (Galison 1997), the influence of lab architecture on scientific communication (Galison and Thompson 1999; Gieryn 1998, 1999; Kaji-O'Grady and Smith 2019; Klonk 2016), the impact of urban fabric, infrastructure and city development on the production of scientific knowledge (Dierig,

Lachmund, and Mendelsohn 2003) and the effects of space on the credibility of scientific claims (Gieryn 2006). Focusing on the local, situated and embedded nature of science, science studies scholars demonstrated in the past three decades that science is marked by the local and the spatial circumstances of its making; that *'where science is conducted* – in what physical and social space – is a crucial ingredient in establishing the credibility and the status of knowledge' (Livingston 2003: 23). Scientific buildings from the early twenty-first century onwards have been characterized as 'performative' machines 'meant to manipulate time and space in order to produce intensified social interaction' (Thrift 2006: 292). These insights on the ways that the material architecture of labs contribute to the modulation of scientific arguments inform the interest in the spatial dimensions of the *laboratorization* of the city experienced in the pandemic. Building on these studies, we shift the focus from the space of the lab to the lab-like settings in urban space. Some key features of the scientific buildings of the twenty-first century as performative machines – porosity, public display, transparency and flexibility – are to be found in the lab-like settings of the pandemic city. Equipped with these features, these lab-like designs became explicit and pervasive factors in the quest for knowledge about the virus, mediated the social life of the disease in the city and facilitated new spatial choreographies of urban life.

Through the experimental lab-like settings, the virus travelled to villages and cities and, in the process, laboratorized urban space in an unprecedented way. It transformed the city to mimic to a certain extent the conditions of labs. It modified typologies. It redistributed power. It handed over responsibility. With the unfolding of the pandemic, we witnessed the importance of understanding the concept of the 'lab', not as the physical place where science is made, but as a device to unfold the network in which the 'balance of forces' can be reversed, a vital setting where the virus is observable at a small scale, to be dominated and controlled. It became important to link the laboratory with each urban setting associated with the virus by extending and continuing the trials needed to identify and control it in other places.

For instance, watch pandemic shop visitors. Arrows guide them through a supermarket, how to turn around to avoid meeting others, how to maintain distance, what to touch and how to disinfect hands after you have been in contact with shop surfaces, grocery products, screens and pay machine. A library reader places her book in a disinfecting machine, moves through the library in a contactless way, one-way systems guide her route and segregate her from others, sliding doors replace doors with door handle, signs that exclaim 'Don't sit!' or 'Don't eat!' are placed everywhere. This lab-like choreography provides a setting for reversing the balance of forces – a setting where the virus's impact is minimized and its possible spread controlled. These daily-used typologies become important settings for the entrapment of the virus. Thus, when we argue that they resemble the lab, we do not expect them to be filled with glassware, chemicals and microscopes, refrigerators and freezers stuffed with carefully labelled samples and source-materials, with buffer solutions and finely ground alfalfa leaves, single-cell proteins and blood samples. No. We do not expect to see this in pandemic urban settings or buildings. The only feature that makes them look like labs is that distinctive attempt to turn what appears as an unpredictable and damaging force – a virus ravaging countries – into something spatially manageable and controllable. This is achieved by carefully devised spatial tactics.

Thus, the factual reality of the virus was not simply limited to the confined lab, to one lab, like the one in Wuhan or in Oxford. Instead, its objective reality was manifestly and socially composed, made on many different urban stages. As an *artefact* constructed by scientists, epidemiologists, public health professionals, politicians and urban scholars, the pandemic made visible the collective effort of staging the virus's presence through the lab as a *dispositif* of control that provided all that is necessary for the virus as a matter of fact to become indisputable and apparent. In other words, the virus did not pre-exist our attempts to know it and control it but was the outcome of this work. Following how these lab settings work in space, we also witness the process of the dramatization of the existence of the coronavirus, and we account for the intense collective work required to re-spatialize, stabilize and normalize its existence. In what follows I look at the practices, instruments, objects, materials, technologies, utterances and pictograms used to construct these lab-like settings as new urban *dispositifs* of capture (Deleuze 1992). Multilinear, composed of fissures and lines of visibility, of sounds and words, they make perceptible an undetectable virus. Knots of an urban network, put into place to stage the presence of the disease in the city and to control its spread.

Following a *realist, a pragmatist* approach, which consists of understanding and tracing the multiplicity of objects, places, instruments, situations and events, I account for how in their totality they contribute to the manifestation of Covid-19 in the city. What a spectacular demonstration indeed that society is not simply made of 'social' stuff but is also made of nonhumans. As Bruno Latour argued in *The Pasteurization of France* (1988) 'we cannot form a society with the social alone. We have to add the action of microbes' (1988: 36). In the same way that nineteenth-century French society was to a great extent a diffraction of Pasteur's microbes, this new coronavirus is no stranger to the social body of contemporary societies. Tracing the lab-like settings in the city shows a society 'in the making' that is adjusting to this new composition of the social, with the virus in it, a society that is alive, uncertain, informal and changing – that cannot be explained easily or reduced to one type of factors. Instead, it needs to be followed as it is *in the making* to be understood. We analyse these spatial settings and new technologies in the process of their making and current use. The pandemic provides a unique opportunity for us to follow the factual reality of coronavirus as it is disputed before it becomes settled and to witness the *social* being re-done or re-set in this process of laboratorization of urban space.

Moreover, through these lab-like settings we can witness the staging of a colossal *theatre of proof*. They aim at capturing the attention of the urban public by simulating lab spaces and experimental *dispositifs* where the balance of forces is such that everyone should be stronger than the virus so that it can be controlled. These *dispositifs* allow for dramatized experiments where urban spectators could witness the massive effort to dominate the virus. The key concern of the 'designers' of these experiments (all those who participate in limiting the spread of the virus and controlling the disease, regulating the use of space, monitoring social practices in space) is to convince others, to control their reactions, to gather sufficient resources in one place. Tracing how they function allows us to witness the work of construction of witnesses and the trials of strengths. As Latour wrote in relation to Pasteur's microbes, 'To "force" someone to "share" one's point of view, one must indeed invent a new theatre of truth' (1988: 86). Over the past months staging various 'theatres of truth' or 'theatres of proof' at various urban scales, governments and scientists all over the world were able to interest a large public in the well-nigh daily drama of the pandemic. Without this double movement of interest and dramatization, it would have been difficult to convince various publics that the virus existed. Tracing the work of these lab-like settings, we can witness how their 'designers' recruited and mobilized a great number of allies, most of whom did not resemble humans at all: materials, technologies and pictograms. Through them, on their theatrical stage, the virus remained a 'reality' for as long as the trials of strength lasted. Moreover, these pandemic designs gained *the power* to be present everywhere. They ultimately redefined what the city and society was made up of, who or what acted and how. Acting as the spokespersons for the new invisible virus, they also created new sources of power and legitimacy, irreducible to political or social explanation.

Following these lab-like settings, these powerful *dispositifs* of capture that aim to control the virus allow us to unpack the reality of pandemic cities. Thus, moving across space to capture the virus, or weaken it, this movement of laboratorization transformed urban space in such a way that it obeyed the conditions of a laboratory experiment and maintained the reversal of the balance of power. The laboratorization of the city ensured that the experiments carried out in scientific labs around the world, when successful, could have a greater effect. Thus, there is a continuity between the 'laboratories' in which the virus was tested, where its 'factual' was made, and where vaccines were developed, and the 'outside', urban spaces and buildings, and the everyday life of the city. The impression of a break between the two entirely disappears when we consider the long, continuous sequence of experimental lab-like settings in urban space. If we follow them, we easily find ourselves in the extended lab that the city has become during the pandemic.

CHAPTER 2

The laboratorization of urban space

A host, as often noted (Serres 1982), is both hospitable and hostile at once. This hostility was sensed at first: as the theatre of proof changed location from the lab to the city and as the city began acting as a host everyone wondered what changes will be introduced. Some cities retained happiness; others endured major catastrophes. 'What are we facing?', architects, urban planners and theorists wondered as they strolled in and reflected on deserted cities. Is this a form of conservation or radical change? Or, of accelerated gentrification reinforcing the 'double emptiness' of some cities (Lindner and Sandoval 2021)? While it is too early to speculate on an answer to these questions and to reflect on whether the pandemic has caused the death of certain urban practices or actors, and redefined the aesthetics of vacancy and enforced emptiness, what is certain is that the pandemic has undeniably triggered small differences in the urban fabric, typologies and material arrangements in buildings – let the ways in which dwellers move through these spaces. In what follows, we will trace some of these very closely.

As the virus began to dwell in different typologies, special settings reminiscent of labs – and therefore, indicating that we are in the presence of this invisible dweller – emerged in public squares, streets, shopping malls, supermarkets and outdoor markets, universities and schools, libraries, museums and galleries, parks, restaurants, cafés and bars, as well as in various modes of public transport. These settings point to the fact that a virus cannot survive without humans, shared spaces and transmission techniques – its hosts – that are necessary to keep it in existence, whether restrained or unleashed. To detect, control and eventually stop its spread, special *dispositifs* for entrapment are needed. Thus, as the lab with its specific inscriptions and spatial arrangements, infiltrated urban life, we witnessed a completely different dynamic of urban living unfold, new technologies and a new pictorial language governed our cities during the pandemic. The prevalence of these lab-like settings transformed the face of cities. Similar principles began guiding urban life, no matter if you are staying in or circulating in the city, no matter if you are in Los Angeles or Aman, Buenos Aires or Accra.

The pandemic triggered intensive fabulation (Deleuze 1989) and that pure and simple story-telling function stood in opposition to fiction. Moreover, instead of contrasting fabulation with a supposedly external standard of reality (Bogue 2010; Stenner 2018), it became closely embedded in the social perception of the virus; fabulation is the becoming of the real. Not a subjective distortion of reality but a means to grasp and enact new becoming. It is not the real, as Deleuze postulated, but the story-telling function which gives the false the power which makes it into a memory, a legend and a monster. As stories circulated across the pandemic city, we all witnessed the becoming real of the virus; stirring the imagination of old and young, it started to 'make fiction' and by making up legends contributed to collective groupings of concerned dwellers. During the Covid-19 crisis, we often wondered what is a fact and what is fiction: is the virus here? Is the uninvited guest in *these* spaces right now? Through these fabulations, and through the invention of *dispositifs* of entrapment, trying to relate to that unknown nonhuman, to make it perceptible, the virus gained reality. All these stories, this active fabulation brought the unthinkable into representation. Placed at the heart of the real, the pandemic fabulation had a direct social relevance as it contributed to the invention of a new sense of togetherness.

In this chapter, we will stroll in the pandemic city to experience it, hear some of the shared fables and witness the laboratorization of urban space and the becoming real of the coronavirus. We will focus on three aspects. First, how the virus has transformed typologies and the purpose-built spatial settings reminiscent of laboratories. Second, how the pandemic has changed (and continues to change) spatial practices (Schneider, Awan and Till 2011) and the spatial choreography of daily life. This includes social-distancing protocols and one-way systems, among others, and how these new rituals modified traditional spatial conventions in cities. Third, how urban dwellers (tested as the carriers of the virus) have become subjects and participants in these experiments, part of its conditions of existence. We base our findings on our experience of these recent events, on the pervasive social fabulation, on the shared fear of entrapment (for in the process of capturing the virus humans often fell into the traps of their own making and got caught in their Covid-19 parables), as well as on socially distant ethnographic observation and sequential photography (Brand 1994) to analyse how the pandemic changed existing spatial conventions and unsettled previous assumptions of urban space.

Scrutinizing the lab-like settings as variations of the mundane functioning of typologies, we will distil some common features that run through different cities in various geographic and cultural contexts rather than analysing each of them separately. Analysing these features closely, we will evaluate how the city is changing and what these changes mean for urban life; we will focus on the new material arrangements and technologies as Perspex replaces concrete, wood and steel. We will also unpack the power relationships gradually shaping pandemic cities and what they mean for rethinking social connectivity. We will trace how many new technologies, objects and apps began to populate buildings and urban spaces, modifying each of them and leading to new ways of being in these spaces. Although there are differences between the individual typologies, we argue that these lab-like variations in typologies are crucial for scrutinizing the daily rhythm of urban life. The variations can be treated as 'patterns of pandemic cities' in the spirit of a pattern language (Alexander, Ishikawa and Silverstein 1977). That is, as common variations that form the key ingredients of pandemic cities. Each variation describes typical alternations in architectural typologies and urban space, inspired by the lab, that occurred repeatedly as the pandemic unfolded and appeared recurrently in different geographic contexts. Unlike Christopher Alexander's patterns, these variations are not presented as problems and solutions. Instead, they are ethnographically described variations devised in response to the Covid-19 regulations in cities, the rules of social distancing and various restrictions for controlling the presence of the virus in urban space. At the same time, they problematize the normal way that architectural typologies and spatial urban conventions function, signalling possible directions of architectural development.

Deserted cities, empty buildings

The presence of this new nonhuman, the coronavirus, gradually redefined what it meant to circulate in the city: whether in public transport, walking on foot, driving or cycling, new ways of *moving* emerged. Since the introduction of national lockdowns, depending on the dynamics of the pandemic, public transportation underwent significant changes. Major cities like London, Manchester, Edinburgh, Berlin, Paris, Turin, Milan and New York became quiet, deserted (Figure 2.1), in what is normally the most active period of the year, the summer months, when they commonly are flooded with large crowds of tourists from all over the world. How shocking was it to see an almost empty tube in London in August

FIGURE 2.1 *Deserted Turin – Piazza San Carlo, April 2020,* © *Silvia Minutolo.*

FIGURE 2.2 *The London tube in August 2020, © the author.*

2020 (Figure 2.2), or deserted New York streets in April 2020! Such a surreal commuters' experience, indeed. Hollow streets, empty tube carriages, fewer and smaller crowds, fear in the eyes of the very few crossing paths in the voided space of the tube network, a desolate city.

Since the outbreak of the Covid-19 pandemic, cities around the world have had to impose massive restrictions on public transport, public spaces, leisure and green space so as to limit the spread of the virus. Many national governments suggested people should avoid travelling within the country or internationally, except for work, education or other legally permitted reasons. Public transport has had to run at an extremely reduced capacity (in some cities, less than 60 per cent than normal) to ensure the safety of the passengers (Abbas 2021; Barlow 2020; Culbertson and Aguilar-Garcia 2021; Isso 2021; McKibbin 2020; Passenger Transport 2020; Sung and Monschauer 2020; Transport Focus 2020). These measures have had a significant impact on the urban life and the spatial choreography of the daily life of commuters (Bird, Kriticos and Tsivanidis 2020). The virus, moreover, transformed the spatiality of buses, trams, trains and interchange stations, and modified the spatial practices of millions of urban dwellers who would use them. Changes in public transport are indicative of changes in urban life and the social habits of commuters.

During the different lockdowns, public transport in many countries kept working; however, new regulations were implemented in interchange stations and onboard the various modes of public transport. Despite the implemented measures, public transport had a massive reduction in passenger transport demand due to a combination of government lockdown and fears of contracting and spreading the virus. Many commuters had to continuously adapt their travel habits to keep both themselves and their families safe. Public transport usage dropped to its expected rates as dwellers have adapted to life working from home. For instance, in Washington DC, Metrorail ridership declined by 90 per cent and bus ridership declined by 75 per cent by the end of March 2020. In other places, the decline was modest, the ridership of VIA Metropolitan Transit in San Antonio, Texas only declined by 30 per cent by the end of March 2020 (Liu, Miller and Scheff 2020). This led to several changes in the commuters' daily routines surrounding transport and the specific practices of using public transport and circulating in the city were largely shaped by issues of safety and hygiene exacerbated by the pandemic. Those who needed to use public transport were advised to avoid the busiest times of the day (7.00–9.00 am and 3.00–6.00 pm), and to plan, allow extra time for their journey, consider travelling outside peak times and use quieter routes. New maps were produced to point out alternative routes and dedicated paths – new instructions for moving around the pandemic city. The impact of the pandemic on public transport and circulation in the city also translated into the cautious conduct of both passengers and transport staff adhering to social-distancing measures.

With restricted numbers onboard, services were required to run more frequently to accommodate commuters while operating on the same budget. If a bus in the pre-Covid-19 era would typically transport up to ninety riders, during lockdowns, bus operators reduced their capacity to a maximum of twenty passengers or thirty-two passengers (the regulations differed in different national contexts). In England, for instance, bus operators limited their services from 20 per cent to 25 per cent of their usual capacity. The government guidelines recommended that people should avoid using public transport unless it is absolutely necessary. Although two-thirds of England commute by car and a further 15 per cent make the trip via motorcycles, bicycles and walking, in Manchester about a quarter of commutes are via public transport. More double-length trams were run to boost capacity; however, overcrowding issues still emerged on tram services, especially around 5.00 pm; in addition, there were no staff members on board the tram or the stations to enforce the rules. Despite the effort to help manage this over-crowdedness on train carriages, since the introduction of social distancing back in March 2020, numerous passengers reported that bus and tram operators have not stuck to their own guidelines, implemented for the safety of their staff and passengers; many passengers opted out of using public transport if they dispose of alternative transport (vehicle or bicycle). Issues of safety onboard public transport remained, some buses were too full and social distancing of travellers was difficult to manage.

Where public transport figures, including buses and trains, have begun to reach normal rates in the summer of 2021, the use of cars has increased since May 2020, the moment lockdown fell all over Europe, Asia and North America. In the same way that the use of public transportation had changed, the streets and the ways in which dwellers moved around the city had changed too. More and more pedestrians and cyclists, but also personal cars crowded city streets. The 'face' of these roads changed dramatically. Major infrastructural changes were implemented – car-free streets were introduced, more cycle paths were developed. As all road users should maintain social distancing, giving cyclists priority at traffic lights, the mobility dynamics in urban spaces changed entirely.

The spatial organization of airports and train stations, those 'mobility hubs' or nodes also changed. Airports were unusually deserted. Passengers had to adapt to new 'one way' routes, and other modes of regulating passenger flows. Hand sanitizer dispensers were placed at specific spots. Extra time was allowed in the schedule to keep trains, buses and aircrafts clean. Passengers were reminded of the hygiene measures – to behave in new ways.

Similarly, in museums, libraries, stadia, shops and other 'public' spaces, we encounter different ways of using space. The library, to take one example, has radically changed its spatial practices. Here I draw on observation of our university library at Manchester. The pandemic library is a variation of the library with measures to reduce the number of bodies in space and the amount of time one can remain there. No longer could the library 'flâneur' peruse the space, searching for surprise encounters. Librarians, instead, went to retrieve the books. Overall, the library was reduced to a desk at the entrance and digital service. The study spaces, too, were limited, in some cases, only about a third of the usual capacity. The signage in the building changed to encourage clear guidance on how to use the space along with new maps that helped users navigate around the building easier – to avoid surprise encounters with anyone else. This allowed spaces to be mapped more carefully so that every desk is given a particular number and is in a different wing. Through all these material changes of the library, each of which hinted at the possible presence of the virus, new routines were slowly introduced into the building. The shortage of personnel, due to illness or issues with training new people, can be sensed everywhere in buildings and train stations. Witness this: more noticeable as they greatly outnumber the users, the few members of staff patrolling Piccadilly station, or the Manchester University library, sharply highlight the emptiness. Physical presence was gradually replaced by availability by phone or Skype. This new spatial choreography entailed also a changing choreography of expertise.

Counting bodies

At the local Tesco Express, a small supermarket, in my village one afternoon in July 2021, I found a special door with traffic lights. A few months later I discovered the same traffic lights system in an ALDI store in the neighbouring village (Figure 2.3). Red for 'wait', green for 'enter', the traffic lights are supposed to smoothly regulate the flow of people in and out of the store. No human time is wasted in controlling the door. This new technology replaces entirely the human porter in buildings who typically has this function, and in the Covid-19 climate, to count the number of people indoors and allow someone to enter only after a user has gone out. 'One out – one in': this is the principle to follow. The traffic lights for some stores involve larger settings with sanitizing service points and an excessive amount of signage signalling the existence of this new technology that is supposed to manage the waiting time and exercise efficient control. Similar technologies have also been developed like

THE LABORATORIZATION OF URBAN SPACE

FIGURE 2.3 *Traffic lights system at the entrance of stores, November 2021,* © *the author*

the Covid-19 Secure Traffic Light Kit. This traffic light entry system manages the building capacity safely by controlling the flow of staff and visitors by limiting access and clearly indicating when it is safe to enter. In the heyday of the pandemic, we also witnessed shops exchanging tips and how-to videos on how to make a homemade traffic lights entry system to be able to control customers entering their stores smoothly. These automated systems aimed to maintain a controlled and safe space, regulating flows and counting bodies in and out of buildings in a 'mechanical' way.

A similar counting of bodies is performed in public transport, to comply with the limitation of people in enclosed spaces. Thus, mundane activities such as going to the local store or taking the bus required advance planning, extra time for looking at schedules, planning and waiting; due to a lack of space, more time is needed. Like the 'red' light that forbids entry at the supermarket, buses would also be marked with a 'BUS FULL' sign, and where bus drivers became in charge of managing the regulation of bodies that could enter the enclosed bus space.

More and more buildings had limitations on bodies and occupants. At the University of Manchester, the library had a capacity of 3,000 per day between March and July 2020, and 6,000 per day between October 2020 and January 2021. Bodies were counted at an increasing rate. Signs in elevators indicated where to step (Figure 2.4) and how to maximize space in the small elevator spaces. While before there was a weight limit to indicate how many people could stand in a lift (~8), now the 'safety' of the elevator is not related to weight, but to the distance between bodies. Counting bodies in space has become an obsession, changing how we think about some of the key principles of functioning of these mundane spaces.

With all these limitations on numbers of bodies, *queuing* and waiting became a phenomenon in typologies where it was rarely encountered before. The capacity to manage tired and impatient crowds (Walker 2019) required design interventions. Barriers of all sorts were placed at entrances to buildings to discipline the queuing crowd and give it a manageable shape (e.g. a line). Special signs were devised to ensure that waiting time is managed, human contact is reduced and queuing crowds can be in a safe environment.

FIGURE 2.4 *Signage in the elevator, August 2020,* © *the author.*

Even the meaning of 'safe' had changed. Previously associated with crime in the city, now the villain menacing lives and urban harmony was the virus. In addition to the many filtering mechanisms of access and the numerous technologies invented to manage access and reduce risk, temperature checks were introduced at the main entrance gates in many public buildings (Figure 2.5). These temperature checks were meant to only allow certain bodies – those with the 'normal' temperature – to pass through. Special 'temperature measuring technologies' were further developed. The forehead thermometer was the simplest technology used. The principle of the temperature-measuring gun is that it passively absorbs the infrared radiation energy of the target to obtain the object's temperature value. It was largely used at the outbreak of the SARS virus, and its advantages of non-

FIGURE 2.5 *Temperature check point at a shopping mall in Shanghai, November 2021,* © *Chao Wang.*

contact and rapid measurement have been widely appreciated and developed further. The forehead thermometer with a relatively slow speed was replaced by complete settings and facilities for measuring temperature quickly (e.g. a temperature door at the airport, temperature kiosks in buildings, scanners, cameras and 'friendly' robots). Based on infrared body temperature detection, and on some occasions, face recognition temperature machines, these new technologies ensured fast-checking body temperature measurement.

As the monitoring of body temperature became one of the most important practices of pandemic prevention and testing, this technology also required new architectural solutions. Thus, the entrances of cinemas and theatres, malls, sport and art venues were turned into *dispositifs* for testing and capturing infected people; threshold spaces that aimed at performing the correct filtering of healthy and sick bodies. Temperature-measuring robots became widely used. As advanced temperature-measuring facilities, these robots were first used in hospitals, airports, railway stations, office buildings and malls with large flows of people, and are now widely used in public places. The robot relies on high-sensitivity infrared thermal imaging technology for non-contact temperature measurement and can measure the body temperature within 5 metres distance. The temperature data can be prompted by voice, and colour warning can be sent to facilitate staff to check the temperature.

As a user, you follow a specific ritual of entering a building. For instance, in a cinema – you walk into the ticket-check entrance, you show your health code and movie ticket, you stand facing the robot, human to nonhuman, the robot reads your body temperature and sends a voice prompt with the temperature data. If your temperature is normal, the robot informs you: 'your temperature is 36.5°C'. And you can enter the cinema. If the body temperature is found to be too high, it will send out a voice alarm 'your body temperature is abnormal!'. At the same time, it will also say other prompts, like 'please wear a mask' to remind people that the pandemic is still unfolding. Its advantage is that it can quickly measure body temperatures without forcing the users to enter into contact with the technology and without causing disturbances.

Between the little but disturbing temperature gun pointed at our forehead and the bulky human-size robot, stands the body temperature-measuring infrared camera (Figure 2.6). Designed to keep people with abnormal temperatures away, the camera acts as the security guard in buildings and could be mistaken for any other camera. This lab-like *dispositif* involves users, staff, the technology of the camera (or the robot), temperature data, infrared waves, temperature messages, pictures and voice signals, special ways of calibrating the distance and positioning the body, regulating contact and interacting with objects and lines of sight. As a *dispositif,* this lab-like setting is composed of different lines of visibility: the line of the body-reading and body-inspecting camera, the difficult to read body positioned in direct eye contact with the

FIGURE 2.6 *Temperature measuring camera at an events venue in London, November 2021,* © *the author.*

technology; there is the feeling of looking into the 'eyes' of a robot or a camera, knowing we are being seen, but not knowing what exactly is being seen, measured and captured by the temperature devices; there is data processing the connection between bodies and virus; and staff overseeing the functioning of the setting, witnessing bodies, cameras and data signals, that all attempt to make the virus detectable and perceptible.

These new *dispositifs* thus also play a role in 'disciplining' the pandemic bodies using various 'tactics' (Foucault 1995) through the play of spatial distribution and the accumulation of time, prescribing and coding precisely all activities of moving, seeing and positioning humans in space, training them to adopt new aptitudes and reconfiguring the composition of forces. Yet, despite this sophisticated setting, issues of accuracy and regulations are raised. Moreover, the relationship between high or 'abnormal' temperature and the coronavirus is not always straightforward; sometimes bodies with 'normal' temperatures are still carriers of the virus, often multiple measurements are needed to identify the presence of the virus in a body with 'normal' temperature and in other cases, high temperature designates the presence of another virus (or a different health condition). No matter how efficiently it detects the virus, the *dispositif* acts as a barrier, slowing down urban dwellers and engaging them in a complex choreography of making the virus perceptible, visible, trappable.

Spacing, distancing

Social distancing became a keyword for public life during the pandemic. Screens and signs everywhere in urban spaces and at the reception desks of office buildings, cinemas and galleries, remind us to 'maintain social distance' and minimize the transmission of the Covid-19 infection (Figure 2.7a and 2.7b). Pictograms with 2 metres and 1.5 metres signs are installed within urban spaces to guide users. Staff at train stations, libraries and office spaces patrol the facilities, like military officers at borders, to ensure that social distance is respected.

FIGURE 2.7A *Social distancing poster, Manchester, July 2020,* © Demetra Kourri.

FIGURE 2.7B *Social distancing floor signs, Marseille, July 2020,* © the author.

Back in buses and on trains, we are all now conscious of the distance between other passengers and staff. The coughs are especially loud. Signs, beyond the coughs, indicate this distance, informing us where to stand, step and sit. Once on the bus, one person only per double seat can be accommodated (Figure 2.8a and 2.8b). The seats behind and next to the driver are left empty. The sign 'Every other seat' is everywhere. These seating arrangements imply that passengers can only sit with somebody else if they are from the same household or 'bubble' – another new image of space introduced. A different perception of society as made not by individuals, but by larger aggregates – bubbles – emerges. The same principle applies to cinemas, restaurants and other venues. In addition, diagonal seating arrangement is preferred (on the bus and train this applies to the person in the row in front and behind) to ensure a larger distance. The seat behind and next to us should be left empty. In transport, no standing is allowed, and if you wish to leave the bus, there is an entire routine: you ring the bell, stay seated and wait in your seat until the bus stops; then you can stand, take

FIGURE 2.8A *Airport bus in Marseille, France, July 2020,* © *the author.*

FIGURE 2.8B *Seating arrangement in bus, July 2020,* © *the author.*

your belongings and any rubbish with you, and exit immediately. Rubbish too, like money, can transmit infections if touched by other passengers. Another host and vector for the virus. This is why additional instructions about the circulation of rubbish in the city and publicly shared spaces have been devised. The choreography of seating, staying, waiting and exiting different facilities is also carefully orchestrated in restaurants and bars, hotels and leisure centres, museums and galleries, office buildings and industrial facilities. A new spatiality of distance has taken shape within a particular material arrangement.

A crucial part of this strange urban 'dance' is the one-way circulation system. Entrance Only! A banner at Piccadilly station in Manchester reminds us. Keep left! A sign at the Schiphol airport in Amsterdam warns us. All these signs indicate one way of circulating in the city and in buildings (Figure 2.9a and 2.9b). In addition to 'bubbles', there are more and more single-file 'lines'. Restriction gates are added, corridors are marked. Two-sided gates become one-sided. Corridor suspensions are introduced in many buildings and connecting paths are suspended to reduce the mixing of users. Entire building areas (such as service spaces) are closed, and their

FIGURE 2.9A *Floor signage indicating one-way circulation system, August 2020, © the author.*

FIGURE 2.9B *Floor signage indicating one-way circulation system, May 2020, © Demetra Kourri.*

use suspended – another mode of being introduced by the virus. A similar attempt to direct the flow of passengers entering a building and to guide them through space is applied everywhere. If, in the past, users meander in space, freely choosing possible routes, now we all follow signs.

This resulted in changes in some traditional technologies. One common change in buildings is that the automated door has replaced the revolving door as both the modalities of access and circulation in buildings have changed. The technology of the rotating door or revolving door typically consists of three or four doors that hang on a central shaft and rotate around a vertical axis within a cylindrical enclosure. It ensures the movement of air in and out of the building. Revolving doors are energy efficient as they prevent drafts and decrease the loss of heating or cooling for the building, but also facilitate the free flow of bodies, in and out. However, during the pandemic the door was replaced with a simple automated door with one entrance, only one body in and only one body out. In addition, the automated door does not require physical contact with any of the surfaces of the door (either door handles or buttons); it is fully contactless, quick and automatic in contrast to the revolving door which requires a bit of pushing and sometimes manual handling and on some occasions, involves prolonged proximity to others. Minimizing contact and proximity are crucial for containing the spread of Covid-19.

Signs and pictograms of different nature support this complex choreography in the city and in different buildings. In addition, new materials are incorporated to regulate distance: transparent Perspex partitions in bars and restaurants regulate distance (Figure 2.10); in banks, pharmacies and libraries Plexi screens are placed to protect both staff and users. Furniture and clutter are removed from buildings to make it easier for social distancing. An entire new choreography of use is in place. Pandemic plexiglass made the Covid-19 world inhabitable through minimally invasive, barely visible intrusions. Malleable and plastic, the Plexi screens served as 'a temporary accommodation, like an umbrella, to be put away when the sun comes out again' (Mattern 2020). They contributed to the lab spirit of the urban *dispositifs* and ensured permeable connections.

Considered efficient at the start of the pandemic, all the Perspex screens used in offices, restaurants or salons are now criticized as not sufficiently efficient in preventing the spread of Covid-19. On the contrary, they could *increase* transmissibility. While the screens help

FIGURE 2.10 *Perspex partitions in restaurants, August 2020, © the author.*

when dealing with 2-metre droplets, they are not efficient if particles are floating in the air. This is where ventilation becomes important as good air flow dilutes the virus more efficiently. In addition, the transparent plastic screens are often incorrectly positioned and could make matters worse by blocking airflow that helps disperse any virus droplets. This is despite the fact that screens or barriers are listed as 'additional control measures' in government guidance for offices (UK Government 2020). Perspex screens only block large droplet splatter that is expelled – for example during coughing or sneezing, which are too large to inhale anyway – but not the finer aerosols produced by talking and breathing that can float over or around these screens. Recent research has shown that the screens could temporarily delay infectious aerosols entering your airspace if you are sitting in a restaurant booth, for instance, but if you are there for a long enough time for the aerosols to disperse more widely within that airspace, they will not be useful after that point (Packham 2021). As I write these lines, screens are being discarded after it emerged that they could potentially block airflow in public venues. Even the ways in which spaces are spaced, and distance is made, are contested and unsettled as the existence of the virus is tested in our everyday life.

Yet, no matter how disputed the screens have become, their prevalence in buildings increased the lab-like character of spatial settings. Controlling the presence of the virus, placing invisible but tangible barriers between bodies and staging a versatile choreography of air circulation, moving bodies and floating aerosols, they also acted as *dispositifs* for the capture of the virus. They acted as settings where the architectural elements played an important role in blocking or facilitating the airflows of virus droplets or fresh air, regulating breathing and floating movements. Reminiscent of the new generation of labs endowed with porosity, transparency, displays and flexibility, these lab-like settings functioned as performative machines regulating the social life of the virus in buildings. Porous, transparent and extremely versatile, through the Perspex all can be seen but the virus. These architecturally devised curves of visibility and utterance attempted to make perceptible an undetectable virus. The quest for knowledge about the disease remained.

Contactless lives

Once you are on the bus or in the shop, in the library or on the train, you are expected to use contactless payments. All transactions require some social distance, some space. If physical money is used, the exact fare is required. Coins and notes are treated as transmitters of infections, vectors, because of the human touch. Physical money has gained a negative connotation during the pandemic, like anything that can be touched, or come into contact with. Invisible electronic and digital transactions provide safety, distance and abstract the human touch from the equation of transmission. An entire urban architecture that had emerged around the touch, centred around the human hand, has been replaced by the *contactless*.

Rail and retail companies and the hospitality industries all actively began promoting the use of contactless payments for germ-conscious users. Pictograms and posters advertising their apps were featured on train platforms and bus routes, at the entrance of each restaurant and bar, in cinemas and leisure centres, and in stores all over the world. To facilitate contactless modalities of payment, different apps have proliferated. For instance, Stagecoach, a large public transport group in the UK that operates buses in major cities, introduced the 'Stagecoach Bus App' that shows the busiest and quietest times to travel. Transport for London (TfL) launched a new app in 2020 that helps customers not only plan real-time multimodal trips more effectively but also be confident of social distancing and accurately assess active travel alternatives. Undoubtedly, the Covid-19 pandemic has acted as a catalyst, a *vector*, in the adoption of contactless payments, and conveniently, increasing the users of mobile wallets such as Google Pay, Apple Pay, Venmo, Mastercard and Masterpass.

The virus has accelerated the use of digital technologies across all spheres – from museums to restaurants, from library bookings to train bookings. What does this mean for architecture and the city? Increasingly, the ways in which people experience the city are mediated through these apps and the 'real-time' data that they gather and provide. For buses, users plan in advance, and tickets and reservations are made in advance. There is a loss of the 'spontaneity' of the modern urban experience. Even when you go to work, a contactless concierge service app can ensure that you will spend your day in a Covid-19-secure workplace. The app can help you screen the floor plan of office buildings, check how crowded different parts of the building are, ensure empty desks are clean and social distancing is respected. Online forms need to be filled in advance so venues can estimate the number of people visiting a gallery or a museum each day. No time is wasted in a library or in a train station as bookings and purchases are all done in advance, from a distance, contactless, without any need for human touch.

In traditional typologies, like the library, there has been a noticeable shift to *online* services. In addition to the 'click and consult' services actively promoted for reference items, a 'scan and deliver service' was introduced which allowed 'a chapter of a book or up to 20% of a book' to be scanned so that users who cannot come into the library – because they are sick or self-isolating – can use the book. This allowed users, instead of having to go to the shelves themselves, to simply come straight to the building and collect the books or the scanned chapters. As a result, the collection development policy of libraries changed, and online books and journals were prioritized. If more electronic materials are provided, less people would search the shelves for books. All these contactless technologies and online booking systems as well as the preferred use of electronic materials decreased the traffic of bodies in space and the risk of transmitting the disease and have led to a substantial change in the library typology. The physical space, itself, shrank. This has often led to quasi-empty and sometimes deserted-looking buildings. This tendency gradually changed the way buildings were inhabited and the entire daily choreography of use.

Alongside apps and online services, there is now a QR code for everything. If before Covid-19 you could enter a building without any prior booking arrangement, now you need to scan a QR to enter and access. Menus, bills, museum schedules, shops, everything can be accessed with the QR code (Figure 2.11). The QR code stands for 'quick response' code, and is a technology from the 1990s that was invented initially in Japan by the automotive company Denso Wave to track components in car production. The black-and-white design is based on the popular board game Go and one QR code can hold exponentially more information than a traditional barcode. While there were different technological impediments to

FIGURE 2.11 *QR code for contactless shopping at a store in Buenos Aires, Argentina, February 2021,* © *Ramiro Piana.*

broader QR code adoption and acceptance, everything changed with Covid-19, prolonged national lockdowns and the closure of restaurants and other hospitality venues. They quickly became popular, and useful, as a means of reducing physical contact and waiting time, modulating the distance between people.

Covid-19 accelerated the QR revolution as the BBC technology and business reporter David Silverberg has observed (2021) in the same way that it accelerated the production of new apps and online services. The typical five years needed for the development of a technological innovation was accelerated to a pace of five months. They are used for different purposes now too. A Stockholm-based company Ombori invented its Grid technology, which allows retailers to have a digital screen displaying QR codes and offers passers-by the opportunity to purchase items right from the street. In addition to being used for hi-tech shopping, the QR was introduced by public health agencies to assist with contact-tracing efforts, vaccination passports, etc. In the UK, through the National Health Service (NHS), designated venues in certain sectors have a legal requirement to display NHS QR code posters so that customers with the NHS Covid-19 app can 'check in' using this option as an alternative to providing their contact details. QR codes are also used for contact tracing, to keep track of instances where new 'social distances' were contravened and the contact happened.

Health checking has become a routine urban practice. Vending machines for health products (masks, tests, medicines, etc.) and health checks were installed everywhere along with the standard vending machines for drinks and snacks at train stations, airports and major stores (Figure 2.12). Health control became omnipresent. In the library, at airports and in large stores, medical checks are done routinely: users whose temperature is above 37.3 °C or have obvious respiratory symptoms are invited to go to a medical observation point. They are directed to the nearest hospital for diagnosis, treatment or required to 'isolate'. In concert halls, theatres and public libraries, for instance, you need to get a health QR code in addition to the temperature check at the door. Increasingly, barriers were erected and filtration systems were introduced to separate the healthy from the infected by architectural devices to remain *contactless*. The protection of life, of remaining healthy, has become associated with this contactless life.

FIGURE 2.12 *Mask vending machine in a shopping mall in Shanghai, China, November 2021,* © *Chao Wang.*

Sanitizing, face covering

While filtration systems have relied on new digital and contactless innovations, ventilation has become primordial: doors, windows and atrium roof skylights of service areas have been opened to enhance natural ventilation. The air-conditioning systems return valves have been closed in public buildings; the fresh air mode is used to optimize indoor air quality. A whole new crowd of nonhumans related to the new hygiene measures has invaded offices, shops, libraries, and the leisure and hospitality spaces: antibacterial cleaning products in toilets and in public service areas, hand sanitizers, wipe stations are made available to clean your keyboard or study space before you begin work in the library or the office building. Comprehensive disinfection and the deep cleaning of public service areas, equipment and facilities are performed on a regular basis. Practising good hygiene including regular hand washing and using the hand sanitizer gel stations became an important ritual for all urban activities, further 'disciplining' the pandemic bodies. The sanitizer became a new object in urban life. Special designs for sanitizers were invented according to the needs of different typologies (Figure 2.13a, 2.13b). They varied in size, design, placement, technologically advanced or simple and pedal- or sensor-based, and became contactless.

Cleaning, spraying and sanitizing surfaces and interior furniture became a pervasive activity of daily life. Cleaning multiple times throughout the day became a constant and visible activity. Normally invisible work, performed in the early or evening hours, has moved into the foreground. Janitors have become 'key workers'. In addition to the usual cleaning, regular systematic disinfection of touch point areas is performed so that door handles, lift buttons, and other objects and common equipment which are regularly touched in public buildings are cleaned every couple of hours

FIGURE 2.13A *Hand sanitizer at Nice airport, France, July 2020,* © *the author.*

FIGURE 2.13B *Small hand sanitizers at Piccadilly station, Manchester, July 2020,* © *the author.*

to minimize infection. The surfaces that we touch have gained a profound attention; they became more important than the human-scale material arrangements.

Sanitation stations became a new spatial artefact in buildings. Self-service cleaning was introduced in airports, train stations and big stores. Cleaning shared equipment like computer keyboards became a new ritual for office and library users. Wipes were provided for users to do the cleaning themselves, which made them more actively involved in the maintenance of buildings. Keyboard plastic covers were also placed on top of all the computer keyboards to facilitate the cleaning of the keys. It is easier to clean the cover than the whole keyboard with a wipe before and after using the computer. When patrolling the building, staff checks that all cleaning supplies are provided such as hand sanitizer and wipes so that the smooth running of all sanitizing activities is sustained.

New practices related to the constant sanitizing fever have emerged as well. Bringing your own water to schools and universities (as the water fountains are out of use) and bringing your own stationery and other objects ensured less hand contact. All eating and drinking habits in public buildings had to change too: hot food is only allowed in some parts of building; in some libraries and offices it became possible to 'eat at your workspace'. You can 'take off your face covering to eat' but 'it must be quickly replaced afterwards'. Commonly open and facilitating social interactions, now the universities and libraries became places for multiple barriers. It became impossible to just turn up in one of those buildings. Numerous rules guide the study and reading activities in space now. Students must book in advance, block a space, take a pre-ordered book, read it and clean the desk after they have used the space. A whole new ritual of studying and reading, indeed!

What happens with the books that the students have just read? In most libraries book return is run entirely through an automated system. For instance, most libraries have 'borrow and return' book machines. Once the books are returned, they are placed in a basket beside the machine. They are then taken to the sanitizing room to be quarantined for seventy-two hours before being re-shelved and staff is involved in disinfecting the returned books with professional equipment after the quarantine and before they are placed back on the shelves. Thus, just like humans, books also must be quarantined.

This new quarantine system put in place is supposed to mitigate the risk of passing on Covid-19 from the book services. However, while the book is in quarantine, no one can consult it or read it and this adds to the waiting time for books, making readers more impatient and books more desirable.

To speed up the process and avoid quarantine, a new technological invention prompted by Covid-19 was implemented – the book sanitizing machine. The machines have been set up for the public in libraries, so readers can get their books sterilized, usually before they return the books or after they borrow them. Similar machines are placed at airports for documents, such as passports, wallets and boarding passes (Figure 2.14). Once the book or document goes into the sanitizing machine, it takes approximately thirty seconds to complete the sanitizing. Sanitized books and passports make users

FIGURE 2.14 *Documents sanitizing machine, Schiphol airport, Amsterdam, Netherlands, September 2021,* © *the author.*

feel safer while reading or travelling. While a lot of these machines were used before the pandemic in libraries, the number of book return and check-out machines has increased since library staff no longer provides this service 'face-to-face'. As a result, the library and university landscape have become extremely machine-dense and technologically mediated, reconfiguring the material architecture of these educational spaces.

However, not only has the 'face-to-face' interaction been replaced with a technological or digital interface, but also all our face-to-face interactions became mediated through a face mask. In all enclosed spaces masks have been introduced. Face covering became obligatory on board public transport, inside interchange stations and indoor public transport hubs and buildings. To be in public, to circulate, faces needed to be covered. It became compulsory – but also contested; not wearing the masks could result in fines, but also conflicts. While the hand gradually became ultra-visible, the human face disappeared. The face is represented differently even on advertisement posters. Behind the mask, the human face became disguised, another barrier was introduced – another small *dispositif* around which the spatiality of the virus takes shape. Barring access to droplets, the mask as a barrier reminds us of the body as a constant source of infection and ensures this line of visibility is continually maintained. Through the ubiquity of masked humans strolling in buildings and cities, we are constantly reminded of the presence of the virus while at the same time making certain aspects of social life absent. Concealing facial expressions, the masks became a barrier to spontaneous social interactions, turning the city into an awkwardly social space.

The new 'modulor'

Managing waiting times, filtering access, preparing and allowing flexibility to plan access and use, sanitizing, counting bodies in space, measuring body temperature, regulating distances and flows of virus droplets, improving ventilation – all these practices have become crucial in the city and gradually shifted the focus from the human body in space to the human hand and touch. It is not surprising to find the hand in the limelight of attention – as a key transmitter of infections, this particular part of the human body is the one that interacts the most with architectural surfaces. Two types of pictograms related to the human hand proliferated during the pandemic – a group of symbols pointing out that the hand is a germ zone and by washing it may become a germ-free zone and a series of pictograms showcasing the process of washing hands with running water and soap (Figure 2.15). The step-by-step details of this daily routine have become a new phenomenon in urban space. All these actions, disciplining pandemic bodies, are important to avoid infection and to maintain distance. The second type of pictogram reminds us *not* to shake hands, and the disappearance of the handshaking ritual during the pandemic radically reconfigured social relations. It was replaced by the fist-bump or elbow-bump or even by foot-shaking. It was established a long time ago that the

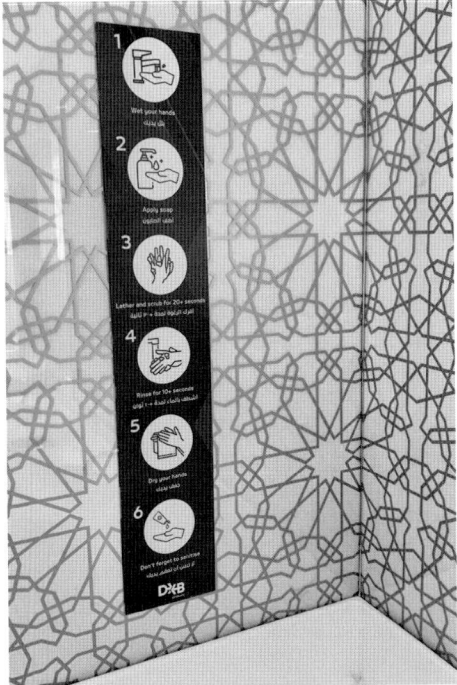

FIGURE 2.15 *Series of pictograms showing the sequence of operations for hand washing, Dubai airport, November 2021,* © *the author.*

fist-bump greeting passes along fewer germs than the traditional handshaking and is cleaner than it. It was well spread in the American context and in informal settings in many cultures. Non-verbal greetings in other parts of the world – bowing in Japan, touching shoulders among Ethiopian men, and the head knock in the Democratic Republic of the Congo – could have spread wider among urban dwellers, but the greetings remained mainly centred around the human arm (fist and elbow), and, on some occasions, the foot. Cartoonists from different countries developed a typology of greetings at the time of coronavirus – the wave, the salute, the bow, the namaste greeting, the hip bump, the hat tip, the dude nod, the toe waggle and sixth feet eye wink, and we can continue the list.

Instead of the modern modulor, the proud human figure who puts an arm up and has been thought of as a universal proportioning scheme that places human needs at the centre of design and architecture, the pandemic led us to re-centre design around the human hand, around the haptic. In other words, the ambition of modern architecture to put human closeness as a basic value was scaled down to the closeness of the hand. The modulor measuring system of Le Corbusier based on the dimensions of the 'ideal man' – developed in *Modulor I* (1950) and *Modulor II* (1955) – embodies a design philosophy according to which buildings derive from the human needs of the inhabitants. This has been shifted now towards the need of disease prevention and survival. Far from being 'a measure based on mathematics and the human scale' as well as harmonious proportions, the new modulor attempts to orient architecture around the scale of the touch. The hand as the included 'third' between the mind and the world is a 'faculty', Serres argues: 'a capacity for doing, for becoming claw or paw, weapon or compendium. It is a naked faculty [. . .]. We live by bare hands' (Serres 1995: 34). The pandemic urged architects to turn their attention to that specific part of the body that focalizes its 'capacity for doing', also endowing architecture with new faculties. Technologies avoiding hand touch, re-arranging the space to avoid and minimize contact, sanitizing surfaces – all these practices centred the design effort around the haptic. Architectural choices shifted around considerations for how to prevent contact. Contactless design environments became so pervasive that dwellers now must be encouraged 'to use handrails' to avoid the risk of falling. They became afraid or sceptical of touching any support surfaces and using handrails, doorhandle, elevator buttons or any leaning support. Strolling in space, meandering without anything to lean on, pandemic bodies in the city became reminiscent of tree leaves whisked by unpredictable winds away from the stability of modern man and the harmonious proportions of modern-built structures.

As greater awareness of hygiene emerged, urban space was re-arranged and buildings were re-architectured in ways that did not focus on aesthetics or functionality, but rather around the primordial aim to minimize physical surface contact. Promoting health and well-being through new technological and material arrangements inevitably led to spatial changes as well as new social conventions enforced by greater control and surveillance in all spheres – all of which were guided by the hand.

Pandemic pictograms

In deserted cities and empty buildings, new spatial practices – of reordering space, counting bodies, temperature measuring, calibrating distance, following one-way circulation systems, ensuring contactless lives, regulating waiting times and managing queues, ventilating, health checking, sanitizing and face covering – imposed the need to develop an entirely new urban pictogram language in cities. The new signage system established in different typologies reminded urban dwellers of the new spatial conventions and aimed to reinforce them, making the *dispositifs* of virus capture even more visible.

Known as simple visual icons to communicate facts or convey messages to a general audience, pictograms are everywhere in urban life. As pictorial symbols, they communicate knowledge, describe relationships, make warnings or offer instructions. Developed by Otto and Marie Neurath with the help of Gerd Arntz, these memorable pictures were at the heart of the 'Vienna Method of Pictorial Statistics' at the beginning of the twentieth century. They formed the basis for a standardized and internationally shared visual language introduced in the 1920s and developed further in the post-war period, known as the ISOTYPE – 'I(nternational) S(ystem) O(f) TY(pographic) P(icture) E(ducation)'. As simple graphics, pictograms speak in a clear and instantaneous way. As Otto Neurath (1973: 220) pointed out, 'To remember simplified pictures is better than to forget accurate figures'. As signs they always represent the same stylized symbols to characterize social concepts, for example men, women, homes, ships, unemployed or working people and so on. Pictograms in buildings and urban spaces are important as they are easy to understand, quick and visually appealing, 'universal', and communicate information efficiently with other means than words. However, like all sign systems, when events take place, there is the challenge of speaking and making sense of the event. As a variety of new issues emerged in the pandemic city, designers engaged in creating new pictograms that address new social and spatial concerns related to the spread of Covid-19. As an international form of communication that can be understood everywhere, embodying Neurath's principle that 'words separate, pictures unite', pictorial symbols during the pandemic became a primordial way of passing health-related messages and eliminating language bias.

The new pandemic pictograms played a crucial role in regulating social life and making sense of the events of the pandemic. Numerous small pictograms and large posters (Figure 2.16) populated buildings, streets and other urban spaces, reminding us of this new urban condition: from those aimed at social distancing (the '2 metres distance' pictograms and 'avoid crowed places' pictograms, or the socially distanced signs of the McDonald's iconic 'M' letter tearing the two parts of the 'M' apart), to sanitizing (pictograms with sanitizing products or showing actions of sanitizing) and face covering (the face-covering pictograms use a simple symbol, but took different shapes). In addition, other pictograms signalled new urban phenomena, for example regular body temperature checks, increased focus on mental health, staggered seating, regular supplies of shops, shifts and lunch breaks, reduced personnel, shopping alone and washing clothes as soon as you get home. They discouraged people from sitting side by side (the 'don't seat here' pictogram is largely used in public transport, cinemas and theatres), shaking hands (the 'don't shake hands' pictogram is largely spread in office and business buildings), from getting closer and physical contact. They warned them to keep their distance, and reinforced the need for better sanitation, ventilation and one-way circulation.

FIGURE 2.16 *A poster with pandemic pictograms in stores, UK, September 2020, © the author.*

Over time, the flimsy paper signs and posters were crumpled, removed and were replaced with a laminated posters and simplified pictograms. Some of the new technologies needed accompanying signage or a series of pictograms to introduce them and explain how they work: for instance, sanitizing station posters positioned adjacent to sanitizing equipment are meant to provide indications of what to do; the pictograms offer simple instructions on how to clean surfaces effectively. In other situations, additional signage and posters are positioned adjacent to lifts to provide instructions on how to use the lift in pandemic times. Large waist-height or human-sized signs are placed everywhere to encourage correct Covid-19 practices including wearing a mask and hand sanitizing. Imitating other bodies, they openly perform spacing. The bright colours and significant physical presence of the signs make them eye-catching. They constantly remind people to stay 2 metres apart, literally crossing their paths and materially creating social distance. On some occasions, the pictograms appear accompanied by a text, and as they become ingrained in daily routines, the text gradually disappears. Smaller signs are positioned at reading height with a stand or placed at eye level. Large and clear pictograms are placed at the entrance of big stores to encourage social distancing while queuing.

There are also giant TV screens placed at crossroads, in front of supermarkets, cinemas and libraries that remind the public not to gather, frequently wash their hands with hand sanitizing products, wear face masks and do more exercise. Floor pictograms and markers lines for spatial distancing are placed everywhere. Verbal warnings are used to convey the main messages and the large screens, just like the large posters rely on bright colours and strategic positioning to draw the attention of users. Yet, in some typologies, the language used to convey Covid-19-related messages remains predominantly pictogrammatic and the simplistic design of pictograms makes them far more effective in guiding users in space – they are quickly noticed, read and abided by.

Gradually urban dwellers stopped looking at these screens and pictograms; they knew what do to. The rules and instructions that they communicate have become ingrained, habituated and embodied. The lab-like *dispositifs* in the city managed to discipline the pandemic bodies.

De-centring the disease

In all these spatial lab-like variations we witness a de-centring of the object of the disease. The pandemic does not stand for the disease itself, but its assumed effects, its perceived dangers in urban space, staged, sensed, prevented, controlled along with a number of other spatial practices. The disease is staged as an event of the present: the result of a performance of 'what happens' and what is sensed and experienced by all, rather than simply as the effects of the virus on the body. The numerous urban arrangements, technologies and pictograms present variations of different effects of the disease in time and space that are perceived, rather than its supposed fixity as precise knowledge of what it is or its predictability as something known in advance. The power of this disease is sensed through the spatial lab settings and choreographies that are put into place to account for the effect on urban dwellers. The disease may well be the same nominally, but in each urban setting, in each daily spatial choreography, a different modality of it is staged and performed.

Certain elements of the laboratory have been transferred to the city – distancing, temperature measuring, testing, following arrows, sterilizing objects, face protection, hand sanitation. The supermarket, the train, the library, the school, and even the pub has become endowed with a lab-like repertoire of actions and techniques to deal with the virus. This did not mean that entire laboratories, like Oxford, Pfizer or Moderna where the frantic work of scientists on the vaccine unfolded, had to be moved or reproduced in urban conditions. Only certain gestures and procedures practised in laboratories were indispensable for maintaining a controlled space. The fear of cross-contamination makes cleaning, sanitizing and wearing protective gear common practice in all laboratories (Novoselov and Yaneva 2020). As these lab gestures intruded the city, we witnessed how the entire spatial framework of social exchange had to be redefined in order to make room for this virus, allowing new *dispositifs* for its control and for experimentations related to different ways of 'dominating' it. Adopting these new gestures, urban dwellers embraced a whole repertoire of rituals of urban life meant to prevent the spread of the disease. If we all keep our distance, if we do not touch surfaces or shake hands, if we sanitize surfaces, if we isolate the sick, the virus will be weakened, controllable and, perhaps, it might vanish. All these new daily routines were performed with the purpose of setting up a continuous displacement in the point of application of the forces – that is to weaken and control the virus, to weaken its effects. The urban lab-like settings turned humans into accomplices. As a result, some social relations were distorted by these lab rituals, some traditional spatial conventions were bent, to make room for these new *dispositifs* of capture. At the same time, new social rituals emerged as well – the clapping ritual to support key workers, doctors and nurses fighting the virus – to help and honour their work, to make noise and signal the importance of a renewed desire for togetherness. Thus, gradually society changed shape to take into account the existence of this new virus.

It was absolutely impossible to show 'society' the existence of the virus and its harmful effects if urban space was not to some extent transformed into a laboratory annex. The negotiations were delicate: if scientists imposed too few conditions, the virus would be hard to capture and control; if they imposed too many conditions, urban space would become unusable, and urban dwellers may object to those conditions. All *dispositifs* were meant to strengthen and extend the work of the laboratory in its effort to control the virus and protect bodies. A theatre of proof, like any ordinary theatre, needed its accessories: stage design and equipment, costumes and gestures, platforms, pallister, lighting, backdrops and balusters. *This* particular theatre of proof needed Perspex dividers, temperature-measuring robots, body-counting systems, sanitizers and new designs centred around the haptic. Thus, the lab settings demonstrated that because of the many unknowns about the virus, it was hard to attribute to science the totality of the force and to treat societies and cities as inert containers capable of transmitting knowledge from the laboratory without transforming it. Managing the virus, controlling its force, its spread could not be reduced to the world of science only, but it required a crowd of heterogenous allies that needed to be brought together from the 'outside'. That is why a collective effort was needed. A massive societal and spatial effort was put in place to help the laboratory stretch its boundaries. A redistribution between what belongs to science, society and the city was performed before our eyes.

As with Archimedes' lever, the lab is able 'to raise the world' (Latour 1983). Thus, the fulcrum of the urban lab-like settings made possible a real displacement of the pandemic world. Fighting the virus meant creating, in advance, networks in which the balance of forces could be reversed, a variety of spatial settings, subtle *dispositifs*, in which the virus could become weaker than humans – controlled and mastered, predictable. The various lab-like settings provided conditions for this, allowed for varying the virulence of the virus and facilitated the circulation of urban dwellers, as possible carriers of the virus, from one setting to another one.

For any form of existence of the virus to be understood, seized upon, transported, and used as soon as possible, an army of actors was also needed. There was a burst, a whole crowd of spokespersons that formed around the virus – hygienists, politicians, governments, disinfecting services, policemen, public health servants – all speaking on behalf of the virus, following its traces, its paths through the city, tracking infected patients and their contacts. Redefining society, the pandemic contributed to a general movement which, like an earthquake, completely subverted the role of some key agents: the physician and the patient. Although glorified for saving the lives of patients in critical conditions, it became impossible to rely on physicians to get rid of the virus and the infection. Instead, scientists in collaboration with politicians and hygienists constructed the whole of the arc that would enable them to create, strengthen and extend the work of the laboratory into the city. The network of lab-like settings for entrapping and controlling the virus's presence even extended the practices of diagnosing, controlling and treating the disease to urban spaces. Large-scale drive-through testing stations were set up in large car parks, churches, sports and arts venues were turned into testing and vaccination centres (Figure 2.17), vacated shopping centres were

FIGURE 2.17 *A church turned into a vaccination centre, Didsbury, Manchester, December 2021,* © *the author.*

repurposed as mass inoculation sites. As the lab was transported so many times, a network of laboratorized urban spaces emerged slowly across the globe. The city gradually became a giant network of entrapment *dispositifs* for the virus, introducing new visibilities and coverings, new spacings and new social relations.

The pandemic thus reshuffled the cards by profoundly changing the list of actors that play a role in urban life, adding new and sometimes unpredictable actors while modifying the texture of social connections. Through this new urban choreography that was supported by lab-like techniques, a succession of mysteries – the mystery of the virus, the mystery of its diffusion – was staged in and through urban space ceased to be mysteries. The crowd of heterogeneous allies which make up the troops of the disease now became visible too. Through the urban labs, these previously invisible allies in social life (hygienists, sanitizing gels, masks, etc.) became an integral part of detecting the virus. Through them the virus was given voice – its noise could be heard.

As prevention and cure became omnipresent, innovative new materials, technologies and pictograms also gained momentum and took over urban space and redefined the presence of the virus, its shape. As the new agent Covid-19 was gradually added to society during the pandemic, it started compromising the freedom of all other agents by displacing their interests and concerns. What we witnessed during the pandemic is a perfect illustration of what is meant by being acted upon by others; what the pandemic made visible was how we all existed in relation to others. It, moreover, challenged those who cling to absolute freedoms. As the virus is no longer a confidante of the patient, but a delegated agent of public health, the presence of Covid-19 redefined both urban space and individual liberties: no one has the right to contaminate others, everyone must abide by rules to protect others. In order to save everyone's liberty, the contagious patient is identified, notified, isolated and the entire family quarantined, in short put out of harm's way. Our movements, our contacts with others are tracked and traced, and possibly, restricted as we are placed in quarantine. There is no escape. Little by little, the disease ceased to be seen as a private misfortune but as an offence to public order, a threat to the social body, and by extension to a shared urban life.

The power of entrapment

As the pandemic unfolded these lab-like settings became subtle *dispositifs* for entrapment. A number of techniques for capturing the virus are used. The first important technique is a fundamental hesitation about who or what is the 'host' to be trapped in the setting, who or what enters and comes out of it. The second technique consists in questioning the disposition, both spatial and social, of both visible humans and virus, the hosts and the guests. When visitors enter a lab-like setting of entrapment they find themselves in the position of host, they follow rituals without knowing whether they will manage to escape the capture of the virus. Enclosed humans and viruses share the well-structured lab-like setting knowing that at any stage, if the lab rituals are not followed, the viruses can spread and disseminate.

Reversing the usual anthropocentric meaning of the 'trap', these virus-entrapment settings gain the potential to influence relations and actions. The dynamics of the agency is redefined. Speaking of 'patience', anthropologist Alfred Gell (1998) points to the capacity of objects to endure action in opposition to the term 'agency' or their capacity to act. According to Gell, objects possess a potential to act, and therefore, any concept of social agency should acknowledge the agency of objects who also act in social situations. The pandemic has made us experience different modalities of nonhuman agency – from the virus to the technologies and materials involved in its entrapment. The traditional relation of humans dominating, mastering and controlling the world, 'nature' and thus viruses is here entirely inverted. If the lab-like settings are made by humans to reverse the balance of forces and dominate the virus to find a way to control and entrap it, when used, they gradually begin to act as 'hunting' devices, as traps for humans too. Entering the lab settings, humans find themselves 'entrapped' in space. Power is redefined in a subtle way. Once in the virus trap, they become victims of their own doing, and the virus trap becomes a trap within another larger trap. A different relational dynamic between humans and nonhumans is installed, a flat order of interfering relationships in which none can take a central dominant position. In addition, the descriptions and the fabulations proliferate as the lab-like traps act as systems of captivation for anthropological analysis (Corsin Jimenez 2021). In this centreless and heterogeneous nexus, every participant is at the same time the trapper and what is entrapped; humans and viruses are simultaneously hunters and victims in the long-lasting 'hunting' venture of the pandemic. Hunting is not only ritually important but also the means of hunting, traps, nets and alike, become metaphysically significant tools (Gell 1996). Entrapping humans, these human-made traps for viruses successfully reshuffle agency and trigger new accountability at the urban level.

All lab-like settings in the city function as an urban net-trap, a metaphor with deep practical significance that asks to rethink the conditions of urban experience. Seizing the movements of entrapment and subversion, disjunction and readjustment of participants in urban life, the lab settings reconfigure relations and dispositions among them. What we ultimately experience during the pandemic is 'capture'. Every urban setting, every building in pandemic times is reminiscent to a certain degree of a human-made entrapment net, trap or snare, able to attract and seize, to compel and capture numerous 'victims'; the urban stage where the spectacle of entrapment is unfolding is nothing but a space of capture, holding victims for a certain time.

Indeed, what we witnessed spectacularly over the past months is the power of buildings and cities to capture different forces, times and spaces, humans and nonhumans. Dwelling in cities gradually became richer, more consistent and consolidated, able to grasp more intensively humans and nonhumans, subjective and objective forces. It also redefined how we 'subjectively' or 'objectively' experience the city. The figure of the *flâneur*, wandering around, experiencing, perceiving and enjoying the city, became a practical absurdity in the pandemic city. The city ceased to be an objective frame where multiple subjective interpretations were possible. Instead, what we witness today is dwellers moving around, slowly, waiting in queues, hopping from one 'trap' to another – following anxiously arrows, looking into the tired eyes of a temperature-measuring camera, talking to others through transparent plastic walls, hiding their facial expressions behind stifling masks, living a contactless life in fear of catching the invisible virus. The power of the pandemic city does not reside in the participants or the formal meaning of their actions, it rather lies in that *force of capture*, the local spatial lures for getting entrapped, the intensity of entrapment, the density of the time that humans and invisible viruses spend together, enclosed, atomized in their 'bubbles', enveloped with masks, and at distance.

Urban metamorphosis: The new technologies of containment and visibility

However, the virus did not simply destroy, but it also *invented something new*. Occupying space by crossing typologies and overthrowing standard spatial conventions, occupying time through transformations, the virus installed unexpected chains where very tiny differences can be followed. Testing and training the equilibrium of urban force, it established a new balance, it obtained energy. Acting as an 'exciter', one that inclines the equilibrium of cities, makes their energetic distribution fluctuate, irritates it, inflames it, the coronavirus triggered a number of effects. No major destruction that creates something new, but minimal inclinations. Neither a revolutionary change nor radical jumps, but small effects that have nevertheless constituted important changes. As minuscule as they seem and as temporary as they might appear, they can produce gigantic changes by chain reactions, reproductions and viral repetitions. These small variations, repetitions and their diversity stand at the heart of the social, constituted by their diffusion, imitation, coordination and synchronization gradually obtaining aggregating effects (Tarde 1999a). They modify pandemic societies. Far from radically changing a society, its nature, its form, its elements, its relations and its pathways, the virus made it change *states* differentially. Parasiting cities, the virus intervened 'as an element of fluctuation' (Serres 1982: 191), putting cities into motion. Exciting, animating, stimulating and enlivening the city, it acted as a differential operator of change. It altered the present state of its exchanges and circulations, communications and technologies, the circuits of sign and verbal language, its entire relational state. Urban metamorphosis became all-powerful.

If an illness can inspire new types of architecture and aesthetics, what kind of spatial architecture was prompted by Covid-19? Although none of the lab-like settings were explicitly designed by architects, the pandemic interfered with urban design by placing the potential spread of the invisible virus at the centre of the spatial organization of urban settings and buildings. Putting in action a plan for the displacement of bodies, the concealment of faces and the frantic performance of hand washing and social-distancing rituals, the pandemic turned urban settings and buildings into traps and foregrounded the function of entrapment and disease prevention. The new spatial lab-like settings made architecture instrumental against infection. Good design gained a new social mission: to ensure the safe coexistence in the city.

New technological developments accelerated by the pandemic gradually captivated the popular imagination – contactless technology, temperature-measuring robots, Perspex transparency, disinfecting machines, distancing rituals, quarantining techniques, technologies for counting and measuring bodies in space. These new technologies and materials began migrating to *other* dimensions of contemporary life, thus modifying society. They turned contemporary buildings into subtle *dispositifs* organized around the human hand and physical contact. This trend gradually translated into a spatial architecture that is about distributing flows of movements, regulating distances, avoiding contact, impeding touch and dispatching energies, rather than containing bodies or setting out explicit programmes of use. The ability to avoid contact and ensure distance in enclosed spaces slowly challenged established protocols of sociality and, ultimately, the architectural concept of a container. Humans became permanent strollers in the city, hunters and victims of entrapment, in need of guidance. Today at each point in space body temperature can be measured by a distant device, quantifying and distributing further the flows of bodies; masks, dividers, sanitizers add more *dispositifs* of visibility and covering, thus frantically spacing infected and healthy bodies in the city. Thus, as pandemic architecture became more dematerialized and more dispersed than ever, dwellers became *traceable* rather than containable.

Just as the new medical technologies that have emerged in the early years of the last century have modified our understanding of architecture shifting the boundaries of public and private (Colomina 2019), these new pandemic technologies of disease prevention, traceability, visibility and distance regulation slowly and gradually became 'a pattern giver' to contemporary architecture. They actively promoted the dissolutions of the boundaries of architecture, the structure, the container, the form and defied all static understandings of space, prompting the development of a new architectural sensitivity.

The disinfecting and contactless technologies also introduced a new mode of thinking about the entanglements (and disentanglements) of humans and nonhumans as continuously folding the space around them. Spacing and transforming, rather than moving *in* space. If the digital technologies at the turn of the twenty-first century turned the building into a flowing hyper-envelope, and challenged the role of the architect, the pandemic redefined these aesthetics by turning buildings into *mega-dispositifs*, porous and flexible, displaying and displayed, regulating curves of visibility, distances, signals, objects and streams of floating contactless bodies. Specific protocols from the lab and the field of medical diagnosis played a role in spatial architecture and enhanced its capacity to act in 'healthy' ways. We began to share the city with multiple new technologies that regulate the boundaries of public/private, individual/collective, clean/infectious, touch/contactless. The obsession with illness gradually began redefining the limits of architecture, suggesting new pandemic aesthetics related to the distribution of circuits of air and virus droplets, the constitution and segregation of social bubbles, the open spaces, the contactless ways of urban life and the various technologies for disinfecting and cleaning that can ensure that human touch can be possible again. Pushing further architecture's capacity to facilitate cures and be healthy, the Covid-19 pandemic entices us to rethink the modalities of architecture's agency in a world of spreading viruses and fragile bodies.

CHAPTER 3

Pandemic variations of design practice

Over the past months, Covid-19 has invaded architectural studios, gradually affecting the day-to-day realities of practice, making us witness more than before that architecture cannot be fully defined and controlled from within, sustaining a 'false autonomy' (Till 2009). The whole field of architecture, from its internal processes to its external products is exposed to forces beyond the architects' direct control. Yet how exactly has this imperceptible, minuscule parasite, this new force, affected architectural practices? And conversely, how did the small pandemic changes at the level of design practice trigger cumulative effects with large social and economic repercussions? Addressing these questions, in this chapter, we will analyse how the virus began changing the state of things in architectural practice, enacted new variations of practice and triggered new types of design reflexivity. Or in other words, here we shift our attention from the spatial architecture of the laboratorized city to the 'laboratories' of architecture-making to witness how designers work in a pandemic social climate.

Trapped in our homes, unable to travel or escape, in lockdown, we began rethinking our working habits as practitioners and the social and spatial parameters of our design worlds. Group meetings around scale models and visits to the construction site became forgotten rituals missed by many. Yet, other activities continued and took on new forms. As we all engaged in pragmatically remodelling both the spaces and techniques that define the architectural practice, working routines and epistemic habits mutated and new settings of architectural production emerged.

Over the past twenty years, there has been an upsurge in the number of accounts of architectural and design practices (Callon 1996; Farías and Wilkie 2016; Gottschling 2016; Houdart and Minato 2009; Jacobs and Merriman 2011; Jenkins 2002; Latour and Yaneva 2008; Lefebvre 2018; Llach 2015; Mommersteeg 2020; Rose, Degen and Mehuish 2014; Sharif 2016; Yaneva 2005, 2009a, b, 2018; Yarrow 2019). These studies explored the culture and the practices of designers rather than their theories and ideologies. They followed *what designers do* in their daily routine actions by prioritizing the pragmatic content of actions and not the discourses. Commonly based on long-term ethnographic observations in practice (ranging from six months to two or three years), they paid close attention to *how* architects themselves produce designs and mobilize visualizations to think in designerly ways.

If earlier studies of practice usually favoured the individual creator, the ethnographies over the past twenty years have revealed the collective process of architecture-making. If aesthetics and art were foregrounded before, the ethnographies of practice have underlined the business, communication and management skills that architects need to mobilize in their practice. If the design was commonly treated as a decision-making process, these studies highlighted the complexity of design as a process of making sense of a situation. If architectural expertise was seen as a mosaic of specialisms, through the ethnography of architecture, the design appeared as the work of qualified generalists. Outlining these tensions as paramount, Dana Cuff, the first ethnographer of architectural practice, argued that 'If we are to offer sound advice about how architectural practice *ought* to function, we must know more about how it functions *now*' (1992: 6). The *now* that I explore here is the very specific pandemic moment of practice. Shedding light on current challenges and changes through the shift to socially distanced online working will provide a critical reflection on the material and social conditions of practice. It can ultimately enhance our ability to positively embrace the potential of a crisis and understand the social processes through which a 'new normal' begins to emerge.

As it was impossible to conduct traditional on-site ethnography and travel for fieldwork, I developed an experiment in distant ethnography to explore how the shift to online formats of working has redefined the creative apparatus of architects. I asked practitioners to 'describe ethnographically one particular situation' from their practice to illustrate how their working routines adapted to Covid-19 restrictions (e.g. social distancing, remote working, lockdowns, travel restrictions). They had to select a moment from the daily work of their practice that illustrates a particular adjustment, a new way of doing things, providing details on projects, people, context, the material setting, space, objects and technologies involved, and producing a concise account.

This Actor-Network-Theory inspired 'writing exercise' involved 130 practices from thirty-six different countries: the United States, the United Kingdom, Canada, Ireland, Israel, Slovenia, Portugal, Russia, Turkey, France, Cyprus, Brazil, Greece, Spain, Germany, China, Argentina, New Zealand, Australia, Bulgaria, Jordan, India, Sweden, Denmark, Austria, the Czech Republic, Kosovo, Venezuela, Italy, Hong Kong, the Netherlands, Republic of North Macedonia, Serbia, Malta, Switzerland and Lithuania. The practices were selected through a snowballing approach – contacts of mine and academic friends working in practice from around the world. Thus, the study involved architectural practitioners with some connections to academia, whether distant or close, and shared sensibilities to the pragmatics of design. In addition, the ethnographic questionnaire was sent to practices of all scales, but primarily small- and middle-size firms responded. Those who wrote the accounts were typically principals and partners in their respective practice, speaking on behalf of the firm. A small number of practices had answered that Covid-19 did not affect their work and these responses came from Switzerland and Lithuania. Fifty-two selected ethnographic responses received between 19 February and 17 March 2021 will be used in the analysis that follows. Numerous practices talked about the shift to Zoom, the impossibility to travel to visit building sites, the social-distancing restrictions and the absence of social contact, in general terms. These responses are not discussed in detail as they sum up several generic challenges experienced by many. By contrast, the atypical responses presenting distinctive adjustments and innovations in firms are discussed at length. I deliberately decided to provide long quotes so as to keep the freshness of these accounts. Interestingly they did not come alone as singular and exotic examples, but often practitioners from different parts of the world talked about similar types of variations of practice, and their responses naturally grouped into thematic clusters thus tracing a versatile web of connections between unrelated practitioners, allowing us to 'traverse' the globe from Amman to Los Angeles, from Tel Aviv to Beijing and from Manchester to Vienna. Overall, this writing experiment provided a way to test what truly defines architectural practice at this moment: what do architectural practitioners depend on, what threatens these inter-dependences and how do they respond to them. Or, in other words, this exercise tested the new ways invented by architects 'to situate themselves differently' (Latour 2020: 71) in the world of practice.

The pandemic provided time for reconsidering the protective measures not just against the virus, but against every element of the mode of production of architecture. What is that we learn by this 'interruption' in the usual ways of doing architecture that the pandemic has caused, in the breaking of the invisible routines and technologies of design practice? Can we imagine how different the world of design could look if we learned from this experience? The 'interruption' acted as a sort of worldwide 'breaching experiment' (Garfinkel 1991) that allows us to witness several latent developments that were not prominent before. 'Breaching' experiments are most commonly associated with ethnomethodology, and in particular, the work of Harold Garfinkel who initially designed these experiments as teaching devices, to make students see what kinds of constraints people imposed on themselves in different situations. They involve the conscious exhibition of 'unexpected' reactions, a violation of social norms, an observation of the types of social reactions that such behavioural violations engender and an analysis of the social structure that makes these social reactions possible (Rafalovich 2006). The idea of studying the violation or breakdown of social norms and the accompanying reactions has bridged across social science disciplines and is today used in both sociology and psychology. The assumption behind this approach is not only that individuals engage daily in building up 'rules' for social interaction, but also that people are unaware that they are doing so (Ritzer 1996). Garfinkel suggested that each member of society uses 'background expectancies' to interpret and decide how to act in a social situation. However, individuals are unable to explicitly describe what each of these expectancies, or rules, are. One way to help make background expectancies visible is to be a 'stranger to the "life as usual" character of everyday scenes' (Garfinkel 1991:

36), to observe and learn how the participants organize their acting together, what rules they follow and require everyone else to follow. Although the term 'breaching experiment' was developed as a result of Garfinkel's approach, he argued that it is more accurate to consider it as a demonstration meant to produce disorganized interactions in order to highlight how the structures of everyday activities are ordinarily created and maintained.

Situations of crisis such as a global pandemic cause major interruptions and a colossal 'breaching' of everyday routines. Indeed, the Covid-19 pandemic caused major 'disorganized interactions' at the level of architectural practice and highlighted some latent or hitherto invisible structures, background expectancies and underlying logics of everyday design activities. It acted as a 'breaching' that allows us to examine architects' reactions to the disruptions in the commonly accepted social, creative, technological and ethical norms of practice, and established ways of doing things. Practices had engaged in devising numerous adjustments, adaptations and even innovations; testing new possibilities, learning from mistakes, revisiting old habits, architects invented new scenographies of architecture-making. These new adjustments, or 'ethnomethods' (Garfinkel 1991), account for a new configuration of relations between humans and nonhumans that emerged when the usual ways of doing architecture were interrupted by the virus. Breaking unstated but universally accepted rules and routines of design practice, Covid-19 newly generated the accountability of everyday architectural practice. This 'breaching' allowed architects to rethink the modes of visualization, the technologies used and the patterns of communication.

Responding to the ethnographic questionnaire, firms from different parts of the globe sketched one situation from their daily work to showcase a particular adjustment, an invention, a new configuration of relations or a new way of doing things. This reflected different aspects: technical innovations, new relational dynamics between architectural firms and connected industries, new creative habits, new communication tactics, modes of visualization, new set-ups of teamwork and documentary exchange, unconventional ways of 'meeting' clients or 'visiting' construction sites, new ways of anticipating the users and reimagining the building's materiality and urban fabric from a distance. The descriptions of architects brought context, projects, people, material settings, spaces and a variety of nonhuman actors together. Interestingly, the designers neither discussed procedures, policies, contracts, local bureaucracy and planning regulations which occupy a large part of their time, nor did they comment on the effects of the pandemic on the staff morale, well-being and mental health. These distant ethnographic accounts rather offered an overview of the local inventions and provided me, as an anthropologist, with a way of 'being there' in these practices. Architectural firms from distant parts of the world became accessible through these descriptions, and their work became accountable. Unpacking the multiple ways that Covid-19 has interfered in the day-to-day reality of design practice, in what follows I will reflect on the difficulties and the potentials that arise from these 'disruptions'. Following the little innovations in practice, the little changes and adjustments, the web they trace, what they do at the level of practice and how they spread, the challenges and little disagreements they trigger when they clash with previous innovations and established routines, and how they pile up and combine with others, we can gradually begin to grasp the complex realities of pandemic architectural practice.

Routines: The 'magic' of the office space

When we follow designers at work and in their everyday routines, as I did in my ethnographic observation of OMA in Rotterdam (Yaneva 2009a), we witness the little steps of making, the challenges, the struggles, the workaday choices, and how the course of action is constantly *interrupted* by the intrusions of all those nonhumans that designers depend on: a disobedient model, a recalcitrant material, tricky software, a difficult site or a new code. 'Architecture made' radically differs from 'architecture in the making' just as science made is different from science in the making (Latour 1987). Tracing architecture in the making is to never lose sight of these numerous *surprises* that continually slice the course of actions when designers interact among themselves and with things. It is hard to imagine architects at work without them and without the immediate presence, the spontaneity of exchange, the interventions, the mistakes and the little steps. Yet, like in many other fields, in architecture, spontaneous exchange and face-to-face meetings during the pandemic were replaced by online meetings via Zoom, Tencent Meeting, WeChat, Teams and other apps. Unable to gather around tables of models and sketches, or walls full of renderings and plans (Figure 3.1), designers worked from a distance, equally socially distant. This was especially

FIGURE 3.1 *Architects from Hassell Studio in London discussing around a wall*, © Hassel Studio.

hard during the first lockdown in 2020. A questionnaire with twenty-three practices in lockdown in Northern Italy during the pandemic showed to what extent this distant design work was particularly hard for small-scale practices. Designers from Laboratorio Permanente describe this moment as particularly challenging. As a small-scale practice founded in Milan in 2008 by Nicola Russi and Angelica Sylos Labini, they work at different scales, from architecture to interior design and urban design. Their projects investigate the interaction among people, and the coexistence between humans and their environment. What the practice missed the most during the remote work is the 'the working wall':

> What we missed a lot *is the common wall* that we used to pin all the prints on. Even when we do a competition, we will print the layout and will pin it, and we will argue about how we will fill in this space with our design. That is really important for us as everyone is around the wall. We look at the project and we talk together, and we can share ideas in a dialectical way.[1]

Architects even go as far as to compare their work to the job of detectives: 'What we do on the wall is what usually a detective does – putting things on the wall that are not organised together and connecting them, establishing proximities.' Now the office is entirely reorganized with new concerns in mind: safety and space. Architects with masks greet us via Zoom, they make sure they stand at a safe distance from each other while working on their computers and especially while discussing current projects. In addition to missing the wall, that precious place where information is criss-crossed and ideas emerge spontaneously at the intersection of two Post-its, architects need to come to the office 'to check the materials'. During the lockdown, they had received some samples of materials, and yet how do you check the materials from afar?

> We had to check them and *see them with our eyes* as materials have to be checked. You *have to touch and feel them*. It was a type of concrete we needed for the villa in Elba [Italy] and may be the reflection of the light will make it blue and that's a colour we don't like. You cannot tell this by a picture. So, I came here in the office during the lockdown with an excuse to go to the supermarket and checked if the material was OK.[2]

Not having contact with building materials is a particular challenge for other practices from distant Venezuela: 'building without full access to building materials is a bigger and unnecessary challenge.'[3] The architectural office remains an important incubator of ideas but also the place where the materiality of the building could be experienced and explored. This is the place of touch, of smell, of immediate contact with the physical multi-dimensionality of the building-to-be.

While architects from Laboratorio Permanente missed their wall, architects from Negozio Blu Architetti Associati missed 'the magic of the office space':

> I need to *be here* in the office, and see that everyone shares the ideas, there is an empathy of some kind [. . .]. If we cannot be in the office, we lose the democratic and spontaneous sharing of ideas. Here *we always catch something from the others*, we exchange ideas, we brainstorm together; but working from a distance *everything is pre-defined* and you lose the spontaneity of exchange, you cannot touch the drawing or models.[4]

When designers social distance to try to escape the contagion of the virus, they also miss the 'contagion' and spreading of ideas that comes from being in the presence of others and 'catching something' from these discussions. The 'magic' emerges because, as designers from Dellapiana ARCHICURA explain, 'we know each other very well. We know the way we speak, the way we move our hands and what this means'.[5] During lockdown architects asked many times if they could come to the office 'just to stay together', an *empathy* of some kind. The missed togetherness is however never about the subjective presence (or even about intersubjectivity). It is rather about the missed presence of a materialized version of the process of thinking together. On the 'working wall' or a 'table of models' the collective brain is displayed. Walls and tables afford the possibility to read the movements of each other's hands and to decipher the meaning of these movements; to witness also how 'something' is being passed from drawings to a designer, and from one designer to the other in a shared space. It is that material disposition of things and the way it is capable of stirring design creativity that is missed, not the confined locale of a space called 'office'.

Even with masks on, architects from Studio Gurrieri Associati from Florence would prefer to be in the room as the benefits of sitting together in the same room are greater:

> There are still many positive sides of sitting together in the same room: even if it is annoying to cover your face, *it is very beneficial being able to ask a quick question to a colleague. Even a banal answer can save much working time.* For instance, from my remote office I sometimes have to wait hours to get a simple reply to a certain issue, because my colleague might get stuck in another videocall, forget our conversation or the phone battery dies [. . .]. And this can be sometimes frustrating and counterproductive.[6]

Designers from Konrad Buhagiar Architects from Malta go even further in analysing the phenomenal, mythical, aspect of togetherness and design spontaneity:

> Good design is a miracle. It contains the geometry that connects the moment an idea comes into being with human existence and individual consciousness. Remote working, a miracle in

itself, still needs to discover the magic of real meetings, physical encounters with a client and personal visits to the site.

I have always been fascinated by groups of architects or craftsmen who travelled, lived and worked together: The medieval guilds, forbearers of the 'Compagnons du Tour de France', the Bauhaus or Taliesin West, Frank Lloyd Wright's building laboratory in the Arizona desert. These groups of young men and women, bonded by a passion for architecture, practiced in their specially created bubbles, evoking somehow *that mysterious moment* described by Vitruvius when men discovered Architecture *as they sat together around a fire in a dense and sheltering wood.*

In the aftermath of the pandemic, this incredible social quality of architectural practice risks being lost. It is an opportunity, on the other hand, to discover new forms of architectural communities.[7]

These very specific sites, office spaces with tables and walls, reminiscent of the Vitruvius-inspired mythical site that allows 'sitting around a fire' and witnessing the wood-fuelled flame of the moment of design togetherness that prompted humans to begin constructing shelters, make architects creative as they provide opportunities for 'simultaneity and exchanging thoughts'. Not just among architects though:

> *There is always something in the meeting with clients that you cannot control or predict,* and it is important for the development of a project. And this something is irreplaceable with online communication [. . .]. We just had a meeting with a client on a bathroom design – to understand the tiles, the walls and the sensation that the walls will transmit, the relaxing sensation. It is so difficult to discuss this by Zoom. *When I am meeting the clients in person it is easier to transmit these sensations. In a meeting they are fully here, in the situation.* I will usually make drawings and will bring them and will even make drawings in front of them. It is about thinking on the spot and drawing and thinking together in the moment [. . .] and developing designs together. It is an important way to convince the client.[8]

The Zoom screen creates a separation, a time lag: when presenting in the office the reactions of the client can be experienced in space while with digital presentations the reactions of the client during the presentation are not as clearly visible as in face-to-face communication. For architects from Negozio Blu Architetti Associati, too, 'it is important to see the faces of the clients; if it's an ugly face [. . .], a face of disapproval [. . .], or not, this tells us something'.[9] For the Venezuelan practice José Humberto Gómez Architecture, this is a challenge too and they witnessed changes in the modalities of communication: 'Interaction with clients has changed and the resources for presenting and explaining ideas are much more limited. It is much more difficult *to empathize with people* with whom you have never personally interacted before.'[10] Dickens Architects from London also echo this argument on the importance of non-verbal communication especially at the stage of preparation and briefing when body language and facial expression add an additional layer of information and feedback:

> Effective stakeholder engagement is critical to the success of these types of projects, particularly during RIBA Stage 1 'Preparation and Briefing'. For example, in this initial phase we usually conduct a workshop with key client stakeholders to establish high level project objectives. This helps inform design direction and client decision making throughout the life of the project. Typically, the session is held face-to-face around a meeting table and we might use 'props' such as an interactive presentation, handouts or whiteboards to help draw out and channel the conversation. However, during lockdown we were unable to meet in person, so the workshop was held over Microsoft Teams. This made *communication much more challenging, particularly as it was not possible to clearly read the participants' facial expressions or body language.* Afterwards I was reminded of the research into non-verbal communication conducted by Dr. Albert Mehrabian back in the 1960s which concluded that interpretation is seven per cent verbal, thirty-eight per cent vocal and fifty-five per cent visual.[11]

The office, itself, is also not a passive décor for design presentations, but the office ambiance contributes to the formation of architectural concepts. For the Berlin practice ac.ka architects, 'the changed routine of not meeting physically and presenting the work via screen sharing leads *to a singular focus on the work itself.* All side aspects of representation (e.g. office atmosphere and office location) recede into the background.'[12] Yet, the office space could contribute to the arguments of designers in presentations for it allows clients to experience the office 'vibe', see previous projects and get a sense of the practice culture. Presenting the work digitally and away from the office does not allow the client to witness the office atmosphere, segregating design ideas from the creative milieus where they emerged and stripping them from interesting contextual layers. Just as walls and tables with visuals contribute to collective brainstorming, they also contribute to communicating these ideas to clients. Thus, being present in the same space to generate or transmit design ideas and share them with clients requires this immediacy of witnessing each other's facial expressions, gestures and drawing hands, as well as the creative office buzz. It is difficult to *transmit sensations* through the (social) distance that digital communication tools set up.

In other parts of the world, as distant as we can imagine, the pandemic affected architects in very similar ways, making them miss that special togetherness that the architectural office affords. When the pandemic reached the United States in early March 2020, architects from the Los Angeles firm Kevin Daly architects reacted quickly. Like many architects in other parts of the world, they 'treated it as a design problem'. Addressing issues of proximity in the workplace and ventilation in the studio, a two-storey warehouse building in the Crenshaw district of Los Angeles (Figure 3.2), Kevin and his colleagues, 'shifted furniture and storage in the mezzanine to allow 6 foot [1.8 metres] clearance around each desk', 'divided employees into two groups based on the projects they were working on, the "yellow team" and "blue team"', 'installed large format low velocity/high speed fans in the main space of the studio', 'improved blinds in perimeter conference rooms so those rooms could be used with windows open', 'installed a pivoting screen in a large roll up door to allow for natural ventilation without admitting bugs' and 'shaded this large pivot screen with a tension membrane sunshade to prevent overheating and allow for meetings to take place in a shaded outdoor setting'.

Just as Kevin Daly's practice in Los Angeles treated Covid-19 as a design problem, Shing & Partners Design Group engaged in renovating their office in Guangzhou, focusing on natural light, ventilation and introducing more flexibility with shared working spaces where casual meetings could happen. Issues of well-being

FIGURE 3.2 *The offices of Kevin Daly Architects, Los Angeles, © Kevin Daly Architects.*

at the working place became primordial as architects began rearchitecting those special spaces that contribute to their creativity. Sadar+Vuga Architects from Ljubljana also reshaped their working space: 'We have rearranged the space so that we can all work in the office, on-site. Workstations have been set 2 metres apart, at least. Luckily, this was possible, although some of the office service rooms had to be turned into working space.'[13] As a result, the working habits of designers at Sadar+Vuga changed – in the absence of the kitchen and it being turned into a working space, they started eating in the office and the office became a space for socializing. Thus, in all parts of the world, designers began paying more attention to the quality of the workspace. Designers were the first to anticipate spatial changes triggered by the pandemic and the architectural office was the first working space to be rethought and redesigned with the pandemic in mind; to be reshaped again after lockdown. The spatial arrangement of the architectural office took on a different shape where distancing, natural ventilation and sanitation practices that we had witnessed earlier giving shape to the *dispositifs* of the pandemic city, now orchestrated a new spatial choreography of design work based on air and droplet circulation and new lines of visibility and covering; new patterns of sociality emerged too.

Yet, no matter how many 'architectural' barriers to the spread of the Covid-19 disease were crafted in the office, architects had to work remotely:

> *Physical model-making* has long been part of our design process and studio identity; through the pandemic we have also come to realize that it is the basis on which we build consensus and a shared understanding of our own work; *it is the lingua franca that communicates across the hierarchy of the office workflow.* During Covid, model production has shifted from an everyday, iterative undertaking focused on studies and multiple approaches to the completion of 'finished' models that no one really finds completely satisfactory. *I miss the routine reveal of small steps*, and the rest of the project team misses *the edits and course corrections that are implicit in seeing the small variations on central ideas.* Collectively we miss the experience of an entire team standing around and seeing the same physical thing at the same moment, an experience we have been unable to recreate on Zoom.[14]

If Laboratorio Permanente in Milan missed the togetherness around the 'common wall', Kevin Daly architects in Los Angeles missed the shared consensus that could emerge by standing around 'the same physical thing', the model. In another part of the world, in Amman, architects from the Urban Planning Center introduced Microsoft Teams, Zoom and WhatsApp for communication and began carrying out their day-to-day team meetings through Microsoft Teams and sharing data through WhatsApp. Yet, of course, something was missing: sometimes they wished they could 'express ideas on paper, print the plans or do some sketches, scan them and send them to the team members as it's easier than doing it on a computer'.[15] For PPAG architects from Vienna, design ideas always emerge within the bustling and interactive framework of the team. The video conference work does not deliver the usual quality and contentment. In the office, architects argue, 'we can *physically experience what we see on each other's dashboards with the corner of the eye*, to be able to address it, to ask questions "en passant" and exchange. We intrinsically need to act as a whole organism, in which the interests, needs and talents of every cell intermesh daily and closely'.[16] Thus, not only could practices no longer function in the ways they were used to, but designers had also ceased to be detectives franticly puzzling things together in search of a new solution, unable to make and witness the small steps, to touch the printed paper, to glance at the dashboards, to see the corrections, the variations, that little by little lead them to new ideas. The incremental emergence of ideas as things are pinned on walls or as the shape of a scale model changes in their hands, the transmission of sensation between hands and materials, eyes and dashboards and the shared empathy were all lost in the social distance that Zoom generated.

Crossing back over the Atlantic Ocean, we virtually 'visit' another firm, John McLaughlin Architects, based in Dun Laoghaire, Ireland. This is a collaborative practice of seven who work in a single studio space with an adjoining library and meeting room for group work. Everyone is aware of all current projects in the office and follows their development; they can hear conversations that arise either internally or externally with clients and consultants over the telephone or in the meeting room.

> Many discussions develop spontaneously between colleagues over coffee or just passing a desk and stopping to chat, so *there is a continuous ongoing feedback loop that shapes our projects.* We combine this informal loop with regular formal design reviews at project milestones where the team working on a project presents drawings and study models to the rest of the office in a more structured conversation. This keeps everyone up to date on the development of projects and allows colleagues to contribute to each project through criticism and discussion. These reviews are held before lunch, and we usually stay at the table afterwards to eat so that the conversation can continue over food. All of this was *atomised* by Covid-19, and we rapidly found ourselves having to send emails to each other to schedule zoom calls to discuss specific issues.[17]

It became difficult to keep up with project developments and this was amplified by the blurring of work and family life brought on by the restrictions on movement. The feeling of isolation – *atomization* – also increased as Covid-19 affected social relations and individualized everyone into their own bubbles, making them distant from one another. The principle of John McLaughlin Architects began scheduling weekly design reviews on Zoom that all office members can attend; discussing week by week through continuous reviews with different colleagues, making drawings and models to present iterations of the design can still lead to a successful project. Yet, it is not the same. Zoom meetings cannot replace the 'continuous ongoing feedback loop that shapes projects' and the 'natural conviviality of sitting together around the table', surrounded by drawings and pizza.

Architects from STONE DESIGN, based in Skopje, and specializing in architecture, urban development and interior design projects, also acknowledge the negative effects that the introduction of digital and network communication tools have had on creative work. They have operated for more than twenty years, and their work is based on the interactive exchange of ideas and potential solutions: 'thinking out loud' and collectively searching for ways to address functional and aesthetic issues. They note that 'creativity cannot be reduced to simple correspondence and exchange of information. It, *like any other generative activity, implies fluidity, but also concentration and condensation of ideas, because thinking together, as one of the foundations for our long existence, implies unity in time and space.*'[18] None of these practices were asked explicitly to talk about their pre-pandemic routines, and yet they all outlined the importance of being together around models, renderings and sketches, and looking at the dashboards of other designers 'with the corner of the eye' and the 'unity in time and space' as critical for reinforcing that special granularity of design ideas. They all evoked the constantly unfolding discussions, refinement and rethinking of design, the thrill of finding the missing bit in a detective puzzle, witnessing how the hands of others move around, catching that special 'something' that travels from hand to hand, and mind to mind, thinking with all the 'cells' of an organic whole. From a distance, these experiences cannot be captured.

Moving around the world, far from Ireland, Spain, Austria and the Republic of North Macedonia to distant China, we 'visit' Shing & Partners Design Group, in Guangzhou, China. Like the other practices, Shing & Partners Design Group also implemented online meetings to replace face-to-face meetings. The meeting dynamics radically changed: 'On the optimistic side, virtual meetings indeed have saved much time for travel; however, face-to-face communication seems much productive than online meetings as *physical meetings effectively avoid misunderstandings*. In addition, due to the different Internet speed between cities, delays and interruptions do happen during online meetings.'[19] For DAR architects in Torino, the advantage is that they 'don't have to travel or to print a lot of materials prior to a meeting'. Giovanni from DAR elaborates, 'I can finish the meeting, get my coffee, and 5 minutes later can restart doing something else.'[20] JK ARCHITEKTI in Prague also outlines the importance of efficient time management within the office bubble:

> I have much more time due to the lack of face-to-face meetings with various authorities – Czech Chamber of Architects, Czech Technical University, municipal committees, etc. It is exhausting to switch during one day from one meeting to another one and to continue without a break to the third one [. . .]. No time for transfer. There is no time to talk to a friend, to eat, or sip a coffee. We are extremely efficient in time management. I switch off hogwash speeches and focus on the topic. Last week we successfully evaluated the International Competition for a new Railway HQ in Prague: 3 days online [. . .], 34 entries, fair jury. What *you practically cannot do is* involve public in participation in your projects, *or force authorities to speed up and have an efficient performance.*[21]

While design efficiency increased, as noted by many practices, it is hard to expect planners, decision-makers and sponsors to work at the same pace, as Jan Kasl, from JK ARCHITEKTI, reminds us. In addition, regular catch-up meetings via Zoom or Teams create larger expectations for architects for the rapid development of design ideas. Like other practices, the London-based firm Woods Bagot adapted to remote working and switched their internal team communication to Microsoft Teams. Rather than meeting weekly, formally with ad hoc discussions throughout the week as queries and issues arose, during the pandemic they arranged daily calls and check-ins. These calls took a similar format to the weekly meetings (e.g. discussing work progress, any issues arising, allocating tasks among the team) but an increased regularity was required in order to capture the discussions which usually came up naturally when the team members chatted in the office in-person. Yet,

> one challenge with this communication strategy was *the team developing an expectation of presenting 'new work' every day* to show progress and their contribution to the project. While this was a great way to see the work as it was progressing, as well as sparking wider design discussions, this was not the intention or expectation for the call and it had added an additional workload to the team. Over the coming months *finding a balance between regular formal calls (where work was shown and discussed) and ad hoc calls* amongst the team alleviated this challenge.[22]

The increase in efficiency and the pressure to generate more results indicate a reshuffling of the balance between formal and informal design communication mentioned also by other firms. Individual calls, emails and chat messages replace the spontaneous exchange of ideas and feedback loops in coffee breaks and corridors that typically occur in the physical space of the office, where all the 'magic' is usually staged. Remote work introduces, in other words, different habits and a reordered balance of formal and informal tactics for sharing design ideas.

This balance was reshaped even on construction sites, argue designers from the Madrid-based practice, Langarita Navarro architects:

> Before the pandemic, any visit had two phases, a hard one at the construction site and a soft one during meals or over a coffee. It was a way of recovering, in a friendlier place, the alliances and trust that during the previous hours or days had been damaged. The closure of restaurants or the limitation of meetings has abruptly broken that dynamic. *Caution and the rules of social distance have meant that those soft moments of the site visits have disappeared.* In many cases they have been replaced by individual meals, marked by isolation and precaution.[23]

Yet, despite the atomization of relationships, and the lost 'soft moments' of communication, the accelerated tempo of work in practices with no breathing time between meetings, is perceived as an exhausting pace of work, but one that also increased efficiency. It put more pressure to generate new work while clients and public authorities often sustained a different rhythm of work. The gains and losses of online communication are discussed at large by many, yet, the gains often appear, too, to be losses: while Zoom discussions may save time and are more focused, they also contribute to misunderstandings and do not allow any leeway between meetings for rest, switching or preparing, as if something gets intercepted from screen to screen, as if noise betrays the signal.

Back in Europe, we 'peer' inside the practice RS SPARCH in Athens where Rena and her team are preparing for a competition remotely (Figure 3.3). A team of five architects in the office in Athens, two working remotely, communicating with two international partners, in Europe and Australia. Yet something is amiss – in competitions, everything is inchoate, new, and time is limited, without a clear working routine. How do you achieve that 'presence' of the working model, of the shared togetherness and temporality in competitions?

> During the first lockdown in 2020, we closed the office and we all worked remotely, so we managed to do our first competition completely remotely. Everything required much more time: the zoom meetings, the changes to the scheme, the elaboration of the design. Realizing we had no time to organize the final presentation remotely, I asked the team to return to the office in the last two weeks, wearing masks and keeping distance. This first attempt proved to me that, unless you already have a well-worked out model of how to organize the design and the presentation, you can only substitute presence by spending long hours on Zoom, and of course working models are out of the question. In simple terms: *remote work requires more time and a well-tried and clear way of working*, which is not always the case, at least in a competition when all is new, and time is limited [. . .]. I realized that working remotely is a strong possibility for certain stages of the design. However, for the concept stage it is important to have the team together; *immediacy is crucial when time is limited, and ideas need to emerge quickly through brainstorming*. Working remotely requires more time and it lacks the group feeling that is important in a competition.[24]

FIGURE 3.3 *Rena Sakellaridou from RS SPARCH in her office in Athens,* © *RS SPARCH.*

Again, that special moment of 'standing together around the physical thing' is paramount, especially when time is ticking: the ability to think quickly together and to understand what each one wants, to interpret everyone's input and avoid confusion and mistakes. That is, a design idea that everyone shares and is fully responsible for can only emerge in physical togetherness, through immediate presence and spontaneity of exchange, and through the folding of shared space, not one of social distance. It is because everyone can intervene and propose little steps, trying ideas but also trying out different ways of working together, that the ideas can emerge swiftly and can belong to all of them.

In fact, what we witness is that there is no one human, no pilot driving this process, but rather an assembly of things, a world of design contingency unfolding in an office, afforded by different spatial solutions (which also happened to be redesigned by the architects). Here, and only here, the models and sketches on the table, the documents pined on the wall, the corners of the dashboards, can all play that 'piloting' role. Driving the process, they introduce a constant hesitation between the concept of a building and 'the work to be done' (Souriau 2009). There is no plan, no linearity. Instead, there is a 'monster' – a table, a wall full of things, a 'fire' – that constantly questions and challenges the agents of creativity. A building attests to its presence through its drawings, plans, sketches, models, versions of versions, series of copies, all together, in these intensive variations. They all emerge in the design process. Each of them has its own sparkle and presence that is simultaneously singular and essential; however, they are all to be witnessed and experienced together. The design concept has no other support but these very things that it gathers and recognizes, assembling and surpassing all of them. All connected to the emergence of *that* idea, *that* concept. As models and sketches exist synoptically with buildings and design ideas (Yaneva 2020), sustaining multiplicity, against the danger of unity or dispersion, the architectural office becomes the vehicle that introduces us to the various modes of existence of that new idea or building. Not a sublime reality, 'out there' or 'up there', behind or beyond, but right *here*. The designer is not a spectator in this process; she is placed *in it*, *with it* and *by it*; confronted also with a pluri-modal reality 'to do'. And that is so hard to watch from a distant Zoom screen where one turns from an actor into a spectator.

It is because of the incomplete nature of architectural models and sketches that they constantly require immediate presence, a possible completion, making architects search and discover new aspects, experiment with new ways of getting to know the building; travelling across hierarchies as a kind of lingua franca. In fact, what each of the architects tells us in their own way is that for the creative process to succeed, more than 'a powerful unifying creative agent' is needed. Design ideas never happen by plan, but through abrupt branching moves, of models and humans, sketches and pencils, materials and tools, connecting different versions together. They talk about emerging ideas and point to the moment when the building-to-be imposes itself: that multitude of things produced in the creative process and the intensification of the creative repetitions that cannot be witnessed and experienced from a distance. They all ensure the continuous presence of an idea, of a building. Moreover, they all together grant existence to architects as agents, yet, depriving them of their often-glorified capacity of being creators, demiurges and gods. And that is why the reality of a detective wall or a table of models, is so much richer than the one of any individual voice, be it a human or nonhuman. And that is why the polyphonic atmosphere of an architectural office, its mythical 'fire', is so precious and so missed, and even more so, in the silence of a lockdown.

Reflecting on their routines, designers confirm how important the office space is, not as a shelter for creative practice but as a facilitator for these joyful assemblies of humans and things, models and materials, sketches and documents. It is precisely *here*, not in a space-as-a-container, but in the symmetric dialogue of humans and things that design happens. Here, in this magical *now*, neither the architect nor those things are acting on their own. Instead, humans and things circulate together to give that building and idea a reality, amplified and strengthened. Unable to be in this *here*, dispersed in their homes, pushed away in different countries, architects practising in Covid-19 times engaged in rethinking the state of things in practice, to generate new accountability. Designers had to slow down, go back, step aside, turn around and speed up, and engage in new compositions. A strange 'dance' indeed! One that required, as we will see, a different choreography than the dance that we have witnessed at the urban scale.

Slowing down: The return to the verbal, the written and the sketch

Deprived of the opportunity of experiencing the little steps and interacting with models and sketches, architects had to find ways to replace this experience. They had to go back to some less used or forgotten creative methods. This 'return' or 'detour' is described dramatically by some practices: 'Three decades ago, when the computer and the new drafting program revolution quickly replaced the old manual school of drawing and impacted the way we used to practice architecture, nothing could have made such *a major detour in our practices until Covid-19*! The global pandemic laid its shadows on our daily routine including our practice of architecture as never before.'[25] The theatrical comparison of the disruptive force of the 'digital revolution', to its 'detour', is revealing for the scope of the disturbances caused by the pandemic in small architectural firms. For the Brazilian practice arquiteto paisagista in Rio de Janeiro:

> The biggest challenge has been brainstorming for new ideas. The dynamics of this type of meetings have changed considerably. *The body posture and the way of expressing orally in front of the screens are considerably different from the previous scenarios when we were all together in a room.* Adapted to this new context, we are usually less expressive.[26]

Impossible to share a table in a room and gather around drawings scattered around that table, Duarte's team had to make an important adjustment in their working routine and began making drawings together on the screen that aimed to reach a level of quality comparable to what they do on paper. Witness his practice 'discussing' on the Zoom screen, everything matters in design communication (Figure 3.4). And its dynamic is so different in the 'spatiality' of the flat computer screen. Architects from the firm arquiteto paisagista are 'gathered around' images on the screens of their individual computers, sharing the same image and looking at the faces of others doing the same thing. The presence of the body is diluted, the corporal posture is static, the gestures are paused and the facial expressions are well calculated. Slowing down, going back, the practice returns to 'primary design without sophistication'. Rather than agitating gestures, abrupt bodily reactions and swift movements around a table, ideas are expressed in a disembodied way, with words and design talk. The precious ritual of collective design-by-drawing and sharing insights by gestures is now replaced by design-by-talking, by articulating ideas in phrases. The turn of a phrase says a lot about the design. Yet, those professionals who normally were intimidated by good designers when a design is shared and discussed around the table, now, at the time of Zoom, have the opportunity to more confidently express their ideas and concepts verbally. Ideas soon came from designers who took a little risk as working via Zoom activated new potentials that provided opportunities for different types of expertise to be shared and appreciated. The screen also flattens the hierarchies:

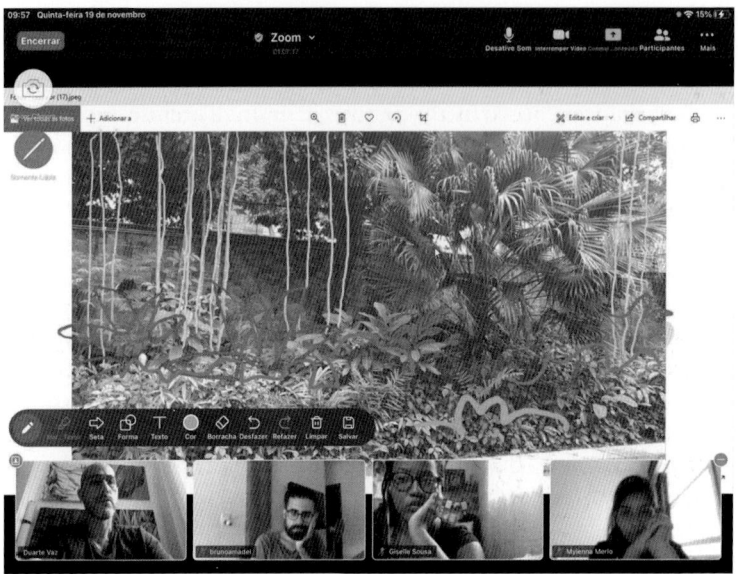

FIGURE 3.4 *Zoom brainstorming of the team of arquiteto paisagista in Rio de Janeiro,* © *arquiteto paisagista.*

Another factor that has helped to create a more inclusive and participatory atmosphere during brainstorming for ideas is the simple fact *that video call meeting platforms do not offer any idea of hierarchy on the screen* regarding the position or the physical aspects of each participant. In these meetings, distributed in small rectangles on the screen, we have equal proportions and weight.[27]

That particular advantage of screens to flatten and dilute hierarchy and make invisible those features of the participants that might interfere in design discussion, that may distract or divert, distort or create bias in the process is an important one. While something is lost when moving from space to screen discussions, something new is also gained. The return to primary, basic design ideas (bracketing sophistication) and the return to verbal expression in design communication (bracketing gestural and bodily language) makes designers rethink their work, along with questions of inclusivity, collegiality, diverse and complementary expertise, hierarchy and physical differences, and collective effort and participation.

In some practices, the return to the verbal is also accompanied by a return to more written communication. Argentinian practice Diego Arraigada Arquitectos from Rosario considers design as 'a result of a set of conditions and information in an attempt to diminish the capricious aspects of design and in favour of a result that emerges from specific data'.[28] To test this idea, in the middle of the design process, they often challenge themselves by saying: 'Don't draw your idea for me, but instead, could you tell me the precise set of steps, information and criteria that support the proposal? Let's pretend that you say them to me on the phone and I have to arrive at the exact same result without looking at each other's drawing.'[29] Asking his collaborators to 'act strange' by telling rather than drawing an idea, Diego invents, without knowing it, his own 'breaching experiment' tailored for his practice. A small experiment within the context of the overall 'breaching experiment' that the pandemic has caused.

The lockdown provided an opportunity to put this idea in action. When restrictions were imposed on travelling and office work, all members of Diego Arraigada Arquitectos were at home. They suddenly discovered 'a great opportunity to test this idea in a literal way'. Explaining design ideas on the phone or in written form, architects tested if they would arrive at the exact same result without looking at each other's drawings, gestures, facial expressions and being influenced by them:

> We avoided video conferences and did a lot of oral or written communication on purpose. Even if it was a very small scale experiment the results were very interesting because this way of working *left no place for random decisions,* and we all had *to distil the design decisions* to make them able to be transmitted in that way. In the same way a tool or technique always leaves traces in the final result, this self-restricted condition of teamwork resulted in specific and precise projects.[30]

Designers from Diego Arraigada Arquitectos point to an important aspect of design communication here – spontaneity. For them, spontaneity could lead to randomness which is not always in favour of great design ideas. Having to purify and sift, to 'distil' a precise idea and save it from rough experimentation and serendipity, is something that led his practice to more detailed design concepts and resulted in precise project resolutions. The preparation process required for verbal and written design communication is longer. While ideas could remain fuzzy and indistinct in drawings, in verbal and written expression ideas get clearer and more articulate. Much has been written on language as a necessary part of architecture. Adrian Forty (2004) outlined the paradoxical abrupt rejection of language by designers while at the same time language is of crucial importance for communicating concepts and for the reception of buildings. He endorsed an understanding of architecture as a four-part system constituted of buildings, their images, drawings and the critical discourse about them generated by architects, clients, critics and others. The return to verbal and written expression during the pandemic prompted designers to think more about language before they draw and act. The outcomes, again in the spirit of small-scale 'breaching experiments' at the level of practice, can be read as true attempts of accountability of the background expectations of each practice. Through the reactions and the responses of practitioners, some implicit ordinarily creative mechanisms of the functioning of the practice are revealed, and the established working methods, hierarchies and distributions of expertise are questioned, discussed and rethought.

In another practice, CityLAB in Los Angeles, the return to the verbal took a different form – storytelling. CityLAB-UCLA's practices for envisioning shared urban futures inherently focus on methods of community engagement, often in collaboration with coLAB, a community-embedded, off-campus centre in Westlake and MacArthur Park. Several months before Covid-19 struck, CityLAB architects set up a shop in a youth after-school programme called Heart of Los Angeles (HOLA), revelling in chance encounters and planned workshops with varied community partners. In the frame of the project 'Banqueteando en Westlake: the sidewalk as a verb', in partnership with HOLA Visual Arts, architects had asked, 'How can design expand the role of the everyday living sidewalk?' The method of 'thick mapping' (Cuff et al. 2020) was used as an investigative strategy of cartographic co-creation in which group members affix observations, data, histories, preferences, questions and experiences to a large base map. The maps are rich, multi-layered and open-ended documentary platforms that highlight problems and opportunities for future design intervention. However, in lockdown, the once-busy sidewalks of Westlake were transformed from a site of opportunity into a pandemic health hazard and thick mapping became difficult as participants could not experience the neighbourhood. Community members lacked stable internet or devices and had trouble visualizing the neighbourhood in an abstract plan. CityLAB evolved workarounds that opened a new set of flexible and participatory practices:

> Drawing from the work of prior cityLAB collaborator Leigh Anna Hidalgo and HOLA storyteller Marlené Nancy López, we asked our young partners not to map, but *to tell us a story of their sidewalks in a graphic novel or fotonovela form*. Our team provided a friendly first step into collage aesthetics: stickers, markers, maps, coloured tapes, and base drawings were assembled in a 'Kit of Arts' delivered to their doorsteps. *Focusing on memories brought their personal perspectives of space to the fore, releasing an untapped sense of agency in the neighbourhood.* The stories they shared were at once familiar and intimate, coloured by a longing to be back in public space: tales of dropping bookbags in puddles, confrontations with police, and crashing scooters.[31]

Reflecting on this invention, cityLAB architects observed that while participants delighted in the kits, translating their complex personal stories to the page proved challenging and so was the process of assembling many independent graphic stories into one visual representation. Despite the challenges of remote engagement, this invention enabled architects to devise new techniques for community participation, in generating spatial ethnographies that can prompt new design interventions.

While LA architects mobilized storytelling, the Brasil Arquitetura Studio from São Paulo turned to the written form as a means of communication and exchange for projects to replace immediate presence and design thinking on the spot. Marcelo from Brasil Arquitetura Studio remembers the good times before the pandemic:

> I used to sit next to each employee with their computer and, starting from the screen view, I would direct them and help them

modify and adjust the projects in real time, with the help of small sketches (I do not use the computer to draw). We can now upload the drawings on the computer and look at the screen from a distance, but *we lose the possibility of dialoguing and also drawing on paper in real time – a sketch, an annotation.* We have changed our way of designing and developing projects. The words, gestures and looks, pauses, facial expressions and silences; in short, the natural and inherent reactions to human contact are now forbidden. For me, this contact is irreplaceable in collective creative process.[32]

Reframing problems and engaging in a reflective conversation with the materials and shapes of the situation, sketching and thinking together through a 'conversation with the situation' (Schön 1983) as a primordial feature of designing is not possible any longer. Digital communication and social distance interrupted these processes, or at least, reshaped what it means to have a 'conversation'. Sharing the same regret of not being able to draw together and exchange ideas between them, with and through the drawing, architects from Brasil Arquitetura Studio denote to what extent the lack of contact with colleagues in the work environment has hampered project decision-making. In a situation of design immediacy and spontaneity, everything matters – not just the corporal language but also the pauses, the silences, the shared and unshared – they all have meaning. A situation also, where computer screens, fresh sketches, humans and documents all form an unexpected creative assemblage, joyful and noisy, colourful and patchy, gradually gaining an epistemic autonomy that surpasses its makers. It is *where* design thinking happens. Not in anyone's head, a singular imagination or on a distant screen. Yet, they do not dwell too long on that moment of regret. The practice crafted a practical adjustment:

> As a response to the pandemic *something positive also happened*. We have *begun using writing much more as a means of communication and exchange*, even in case of projects. I feel that it has been more precise, synthetic and objective. And this practice confirms that architecture does not only have the field of drawing as its representative language. *It is richer. It can be done by other languages, and writing is one of them.*[33]

As in the practices arquiteto paisagista and Diego Arraigada Arquitectos where the immediate presence of the body in design communication was compensated and replaced by more verbal and written expression and communication, Brasil Arquitetura Studio focused on writing precise and synthetic descriptions of design projects and ideas. If we were to follow designers from these practices as they draw and talk about design, this close anthropological look will demonstrate the circularity and contingency of speech. Yet, they write. It is in the nature of language that words are written in a linear way and thus more precision and details could be achieved. If language implies more linearity and projectability, even objectivity, as Diego suggests, drawings require immediacy, spontaneity, circularity, flexibility as well as multiple perspectives and interpretability. This new effort in practices that consists in thinking more *before* doing, better articulating *before* expressing, conceptualizing and projecting *before* sketching, might have looked impossible before the pandemic, radically 'breaching' shared expectations in their design work. As Forty demonstrated when tracing the relationship between drawing, language and ideas, the thinking that architecture might be projected not in drawings but entirely in words, has always been a possibility. He reminded us of the Italian group Archizoom and their scheme for verbal descriptions presented in the late 1960s and the fact that renowned architects like William Alsop and Jean Nouvel have made notable projects in words. The pandemic response of architects revives the relevance of these historical examples for contemporary practitioners and reinforces Adolf Loos' belief that 'good architecture, how something is to be built, can be written' (1924: 139). It intersects with other arguments from the responses of the designers, namely, the concern that informal design communications have suffered as they gained a degree of formality and the importance to think carefully about the steps to take before taking them, to preprepare, to plan and pre-plan. In fact, it is not by chance that practices often use the prefix 'pre-' to describe their work; the linearity of 'pre-' reinforces the logic and temporality of language.

In this extreme pandemic situation of practice language and writing are considered by practitioners as more articulate and more precise than drawing, contrary to Otto Neurath's belief that words are ambiguous and easily misunderstood. Rethinking their practice now, architects slow down and go back to some traditional forms of design communication and expression. Traditional but not completely new and surprising. It might be even argued that buildings are more like language than drawings as they cannot be experienced at once, but step by step, by moving through. This sequential motion is much more easily represented by language than it is by drawing as when we 'read a drawing', we are 'projecting imagined bodily movements around a drawn plan or section' (Forty 2004: 39); this language-like act of interpretation impacts more directly the mind than any images or drawings that can be interpreted in different ways and from multiple perspectives.

In addition, as designers from Brasil Arquitetura Studio remind us, architecture cannot be reduced to drawings only; it includes a variety of forms of expressions, many different languages, both visual and textual. The pandemic made visible again this richness of architectural media, which was there before, but whose potential was somehow taken for granted, or negated.

Back in Europe, in Italy, architects express a very similar change. While most of them regret the loss of spontaneous gatherings around models and sketches, that spur-of-the-moment exchange, for some 'the new condition of isolation – reduction of meetings, calls, distractions of all kinds – has *improved the quality of time to reflect on projects*'.[34] The constraints and limitations imposed by the pandemic and the numerous lockdowns also offer new opportunities: to gain more time to think, process, reflect, write and capitalize on what has been done, consolidating the achievements of the practice. Not being able to share one space had some advantages for architects from Negozio Blu Architetti too: 'it has redefined the roles and responsibilities in the team', and principles 'had to delegate more responsibilities to the collaborators'.[35] Nicola from Laboratorio Permanente also foregrounds this change. He found out that 'writing worked better during lockdown' and took the time to think about what he was writing. Moreover, he started to delegate writing responsibilities to his younger colleagues. Writing in the office, in the middle of a hectic design rhythm, is not always efficient: 'writing worked better during lockdown. My junior collaborators *took the time to think about what they were writing* as writing in the office is not good. When you are alone in your office looking at the landscape [. . .] you write much better.'[36] Thus, while some architects spent time mourning the loss of the 'office magic', others contemplated the time, richness and depth gained in isolation. While remote discussions with partners were still possible and had led to efficient work processes, discussing with close collaborators required a redefinition of the roles. Architects from Land+Civilization Compositions tell a similar story of reshuffled roles and a changing dynamic of trust delegation:

> For our work the necessity of the digital interface brought on by Covid, ironically has made our office have a more personal connection to the work, clients and users. To explain, I must give some context to our working reality. We previously were primarily based in Hong Kong, but most of the projects were in Shenzhen. And, as the head and therefore 'the face' of the practice, clients would insist on myself joining the meeting, which involves crossing an international border. Of course, as someone who sadly cannot speak either Cantonese or Mandarin, this always still entailed a staff member joining, who often was treated more as 'just a translator'.
>
> As the realities of the virus set in, a few of our HK team volunteered to shift their living realities temporarily to Shenzhen in order to carry on more conveniently with our work. But as time went along, their presence became less of a matter of convenience, and more that of necessity. Slowly I, my team, and the clients adapted to the reality of me joining meetings via whatever-digital-video-interface. And as time went further along, the necessity for me to join the meetings drifted further and further away.
>
> *In reality, what Covid did for our work was force my younger staff to take charge and not rely on me.* It forced our clients to realize the symbolic presence of 'the boss' is often overrated. And allowed me not to just spend less time travelling to and from meetings, *but allowed me to delegate more, to trust more, and often learn more.*
>
> Now, this accepted way of working is just the norm in our practice. The team leaders set up meetings, talk to clients, lead with their ideas, and I certainly play a role – but more as an editor or perhaps as an idea generator or at times 'the old guy who can share other examples'. But the project leaders and design staff have strong ties to the clients, construction teams, and users.[37]

As the Covid-19 crisis has led to some reshuffling of roles and responsibilities in practice, the boundaries between the designers and clients' offices became more blurred too. The hierarchies between young and old, the more experienced and the less experienced, designers and writers, thinkers and makers were flattened, and trust was delegated to the younger staff, to architects with unconventional ideas, slightly different expertise and attitude to risk-taking. Yet, architects did not comment on any issues related to increased inequalities in terms of meeting structures, work-life balance or home-schooling; these issues were only raised in the architectural discourse as seen in the semantic map.

To be able to complete the construction of a small project called 'A Moulting Flat' in 2020, architects from Husos architects in Madrid had to gather the dispersed collaborators from several places (Cyprus, Canada, Spain and Belgium) as most of them returned to their home countries at the start of the pandemic. Reflecting on the difference between remote design work and spontaneous exchange in the office, they elaborate:

> In this new configuration, we were located across several time zones, beyond the usual locations of Colombia and Spain. The fact that we could only work and meet online made it even more important to *establish protocols that were less improvised and better planned*. We had to agree in advance on when, how and how long we should meet. The spontaneity that being together in the same space allows for contrasted strongly with online processes, which are more rigid.[38]

Thus, online working introduced rigidity, formality and required precise planning, especially during the construction phase. Other architects from other contexts echo this sentiment. DAR architects in Turin explain that when they have a meeting by Skype, they tend 'to fix the duration, the topic, the timing, everything' and therefore, 'you don't have the gestures of a live meeting, with all the greeting rituality'.[39] If the formal exchange has continued following similar standards of the pre-pandemic era, the informal communications have suffered as they gained a degree of formality. This argument is echoed by many other firms. Formal informality, we might argue, became a new phenomenon in the pandemic. For designers from Husos architects, it became more and more frequent to end up

PANDEMIC VARIATIONS OF DESIGN PRACTICE 113

working in their free time. As Jeremy – an architect on the team – was in Toronto, they began having working meetings in the evening time in Spain so that Jeremy could keep his local office hours. The working day became longer for Diego and Camilo in Madrid and the other members of the team based in Europe.

Over time, we were obliged to find other ways to take care of ourselves and each other, preserve our time off, and get better at listening and taking notes. For all of us, being able to work more independently became fundamental. In this new way of working and collaborating, it was key to be able to perform tasks for each project independently and *put them in common* afterwards.

The spontaneous exchange of ideas and processes among the five or six of us, which would usually take place naturally as we worked alongside each other, became increasingly difficult. Our picnic lunches on Fridays at the park became the only spaces of physical encounter, and as the colder months arrived, they were cancelled. We still haven't been able to take up this habit again. *We created a channel on Slack called #random in order to simulate a space for spontaneous exchange and make team video calls and meetings.* Still, this is far from being the space of exchange that is built through physical space.[40]

The new situation of remote work requires architects to plan and predict more and establish protocols. And in this process, spontaneity and serendipity are lost. In addition, architects remained architects even in the digital realm. They began crafting online spaces for spontaneous discussions and chats to replace the missed physical spaces for immediacy and exchange. The architects' efforts to create online versions of what they have missed, like the channel on Slack called #random in Husos' practice, to simulate a space for spontaneous exchange, extended further the designers' creativity to more spheres, crafting more spaces.

The architectural studio STONE DESIGN shared a very similar concern. As their normal way of functioning was interrupted during the pandemic, it became increasingly difficult to 'put things in common':

What has changed our habits and ways of working in the past year due to pandemic and global circumstances is primarily *the pre-preparation process*, i.e. the creative process of thinking, *as we were forced to separate it from the execution of projects and master plans*. All this led to extended design deadlines and difficult implementation of projects. In addition to the fact that the creative team and the employed engineers function separately, the circumstances for communication with the investors are also difficult, i.e. the commissions and the presentations of projects, they all take place now through virtual communication.[41]

Regretting the lost immediacy, the 'thinking together' in time and space, and the condensation of ideas that emerges from this immediacy, during the pandemic architects slow down, prepare more – even preprepare – and think carefully about the steps to take before taking them. An acute time awareness and reflexivity, running back and forth, requires designers to ponder more and deliberate cautiously on what will follow tomorrow, than to plunge delightfully into the intensity of the designerly *now*.

If some practices returned to verbal and written forms of expressing design, planning more before doing, other firms returned to sketching. Architects from Jordan described how instead of sketching on paper they used 'software such as sketch up and AutoCAD'.[42] Rasha from the Architectural Division of the CC GROUP in Amman noted: 'it wasn't quick though, but it served the desired purpose'.[43] Another practice, Atelier TeamMinus from Beijing returned to sketching too. But what kind of sketching? Although they had to communicate through Zoom, they still 'wanted to keep the same active emotion' to stimulate creativity during the brainstorming phase:

> In our daily practice, the hand sketch plays the most curial role for us to communicate a design or a spatial idea as well as to modify a previous one, in a short time. It also evokes our passion to create, helps us associate with memories. *To realize the same quality of hand sketching, we bought several Wacom tablets and distributed them to designers in different places. By using the annotation function of Zoom, we then could do hand sketching on the shared screen, which means that no matter if it's a plan in AutoCAD or a 3D model in SketchUp, everyone in the design group can add their drawings on it simultaneously and modify them quickly.*[44]

Like other practices, designers from Atelier TeamMinus normally print out their plans or perspectives of 3D models, pin them on a whiteboard, and then start drawing. Working on the bidding for an International Student Centre project through the Zoom annotation function and the tablet to test and explore ideas, they realized that the brainstorming process can be smoother since they do not have to print out visuals and wait for them to print. For example, if they wish to discuss another perspective of a 3D model, the waiting time – of going to the printer, waiting for it to print, return to the table and so on – sometimes disrupts the continuous thought process. The printing quality sometimes may also fade the quality of a dynamic rendered model. Although using Wacom via a particular software still brings the obstacle of software transition, they realized that this new mode of online hand sketching with a digital pen discovered during quarantine could help them to optimize the speed of design and ensure an uninterrupted design process.

Similarly, Mark Foster Gage Architects works with very complex and high-resolution 3D models in their NYC office. Some of these are very large (ten to twenty gigabytes), and there are very few computers that can work with them because of their complexity. As a result, for this practice:

> It's with some rather staggering irony that the innovation that's best helped us cope with Covid is *the re-introduction of extensive hand drawing into our design process*. Hand drawing on a Wacom digital screen has become a light shorthand that allows us to work on the same project, simultaneously and around the world – but using multiple digital models.[45]

Here they are working on a huge (US$500 million) multi-use residential, commercial and public development in Omaha, Nebraska called 'The Crossroads' (Figure 3.5). The practice would normally maintain a single digital master model that contains everyone's work at various scales. Architects would upload into this master model, on the office server so they could see each other's work and the project 'across scales in the same massive model'. However, now, during the lockdown, they tend to be working only on single scales of the problem; one person works on master planning while another works on signage designs and branding. The overall design, then, is compiled at the end through a folder

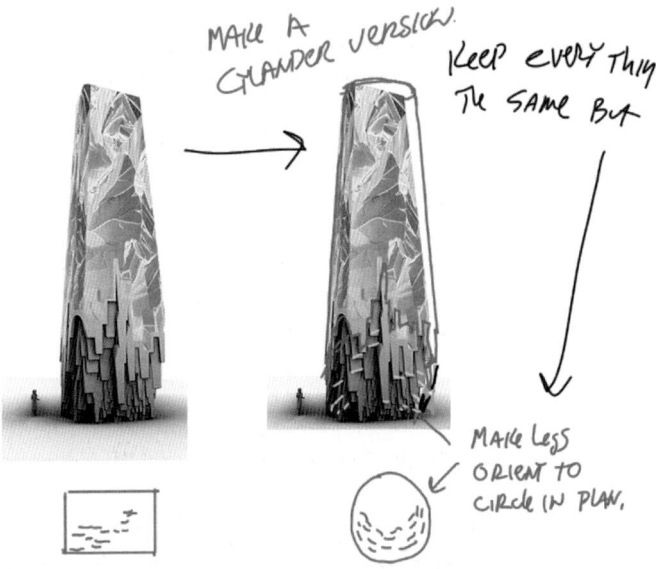

FIGURE 3.5 *Hand sketching at Mark Gage architects,* © *Mark Gage architects.*

of jpegs with the latest designs at each scale, but with the original models that made those images spread out over three continents. Thus, their 'hi-tech solution' to working on projects of staggering complexity during the pandemic, twenty-four hours a day and over three continents, consisted in the *digitally empowered use of hand drawing*. Ironically, the founder of the practice Mark Gage started in architecture as a watercolour renderer in the office of Robert A. M. Stern architects and has a background in working extensively with his hands, then moved to entirely using rendering software over the past two decades. We could say that Mark's career followed what is known as the first digital turn in architecture. Yet, the move to digitally enhanced use of sketching during the pandemic, combining hand drawings and new software, signals for another change in drawing practices where the little steps are lost and the multi-scalar designs risk being 'flattened'.

Just like in Mark Foster Gage Architects in New York City where designers cannot any longer share the massive digital master model, in distant Wellington architects are unable to share the same computer screen any longer as they used to do before Covid-19 (Figure 3.6a). Designers from Athfield Architects in Wellington explain: 'To replicate the scenario of being around a table with drawings, pens and around a computer screen, we started using screen sharing where each person could "take the pen" and "scribble" on the shared image.'[46] (Figure 3.6b). Like in the practices in Jordan, Beijing and NYC, this graphic method allowed Wellington architects to begin 'sharing the electronic pen' while they were all working from home and looking at the same images on their respective screens. Being able to do this and, in a way, simultaneously draw and refine the design had helped architects maintain some form of togetherness, of putting in common. Using the same software allowed Wellington architects to 'still design together' as they had done in the studio and to build trust. The screen and pen sharing brought them together

FIGURE 3.6A *Group meeting of architects from Athfield Architects via screensharing during the pandemic,* © *Athfield Architects.*

FIGURE 3.6B *Group meeting of architects from Athfield Architects in Wellington before the pandemic,* © *Athfield Architects.*

in a simulated space and produced an equivalent of the office. Thus, through the ethnographic accounts of all these practices we witness a reshuffle of agency – previously shared with software/drawing hands/computer screens, design agency is now shared with digitally mediated sketching; a new redistribution of roles is at stake.

Can this reshuffling of agency be compared to the 1980s when AutoCAD software for 2D and 3D design and drafting was implemented and has since become the industry standard for the production of architectural graphics? As digital versions of hand drafting, 2D CAD applications have recreated the drafting table into digital space. The introduction of AutoCAD has triggered a substantial shift in the architectural industry and design education (Brown 2009) and its implementation has changed the status of architectural representation and the office culture (Bruegmann 1989; Lebahar 1983; McCullough, Mitchell and Purcell 1990). Are the stories told by some practices during the pandemic signalling a return to the drafting table – back to the digital transplantation of the result into a simulated drafting space? Will this result in a change in perception of buildings as the architectural skill of imagining the building from the plane of the 2D surface radically differs from spatial thinking in 3D modelling? While we cannot make any predictions, what is certain is that this shift from flat screens to the flat planes of Wacom sketching is already modifying the working culture of designing architects.

Another common aspect is that the 'returns' are related to the shared concern of 'patchwork'. As Husos architects argued, it became fundamental to work more independently, to perform tasks for each project independently and then collate them together afterward. This is something echoed by Mark Gage's practices which we have witnessed working on different scales and then assembling and patching all scales together. Atomising the process of design appears again as a dimension here. Atomization of design tasks performed in isolation is followed by assembly and the final outcome emerges as a well-crafted, preplanned and carefully compiled hodgepodge of atomized parts. That is a radically different process compared to the symmetric dance of humans and things that unfolds in an office, spontaneously and seamlessly granting reality to a building.

In all these practices an immediate response to the pandemic was to go back, slow done and delegate more to verbal expression, writing and sketching. How are all these somewhat forgotten, or we might say obsolete, techniques of writing and talking changing the craft of the architect? These returns make the distinction between perfectionism and good craftsmanship even more relevant in today's context, a distinction so eloquently recounted by Richard Sennett (2008) through a historical example. The drive to produce exact calculations, proportions and floor slabs, and to abide by proportions with formal rules could turn architects into obsessive perfectionists. The philosopher Ludwig Wittgenstein was one of them, and the perfectionist design of the House on Kundmanngasse, Vienna (1927–9) that he had sought for his sister had 'sickened the house', argued Sennett (2008: 257), a complete obsession. This became possible also due to the lack of constraints – he had unlimited resources, time and possibilities. At the same time, in another part of the early century Vienna, Adolf Loos designed and built the acclaimed Villa Moller (1927–8), a house that exemplifies a radically different attitude to design, embodying a creative dialogue between form and error. As a good craftsman, Loos understood the importance of a playful attitude to drawing, experimenting with different window shapes, shifting lights and other design aspects – trying out, not knowing where he was going. Moreover, as Sennet reminds us, the good craftsman 'places positive value on constraints and contingency' (2008: 262); each of the problems he encountered including budget concerns was turned into opportunities. Instead of pursuing the problem of proportions and measures relentlessly, like Wittgenstein, Loos accepted the incompleteness of the work. While Wittgenstein's obsession with perfection ruined the house, as a good designer, Loos knew when to stop so that the work would remain open.

The pandemic revives the profile of the perfectionist, of the calculative architect, the pensive one, the reflexive one, who just like Wittgenstein thinks more than acts, and thinks and writes *before* acting, not because the action is negated but because it is temporary paused. If more is delegated to verbal and written expression, if ideas should be clearly formulated and precisely articulated beforehand, endorsing the somewhat forgotten drive to perfectionism, this inevitably leads us to rethink the craft of designing, quality-driven work and expertise in architecture. In this situation of arrested making, what happens with accidents, constraints, failure and all these unpredictable events in the course of the design process, which, all together in a joyful immediacy, can often change the course of design for good? If the pandemic freed designers from rigid and burdensome hierarchies, unlocked the hidden potential of the youngest, turned the makers into writers, the shy into vocal, the underrepresented into visible and present, will these reshaped team dynamics lead to different design works?

This leaves us wondering about the nature of designs generated during the pandemic: if all these changes do result in more precise buildings, deprived of playfulness and randomness, will they provide more resourceful solutions to complex problems? As Dana Cuff notes, 'this flatness of shapes, these composite buildings are distinctive for the pandemics. Maybe we will be walking in cities in the future, and we will be guessing what was designed with 2D visuals, and on the flat screens during the pandemic and what was not.'[47] As thought provocative as Cuff's statement might be, the data collected from practices does not allow us to speculate further on the 'pandemic type' of buildings generated during the crisis and to establish an unequivocal connection between the design process and design outcomes. Yet, we can question if 'the returns' resulted in resourceful solutions and generated novel design concepts, if the small 'breaching experiments' architects devised contributed to a more productive working climate and changed everyday design activities in a durable way, if the adjustments were made long-lasting. Or was it difficult to retain the effects of 'breaching'? What we can say with certainty is that 'the returns' triggered small differences in the working equilibrium of each practice and helped them rethink their hitherto invisible working habits, made them question the unquestionable, the 'ticks' and tricks, and eventually regain new energy.

Moreover, these returns do not signal in any way a reversal or a rejection of the digital turn. For instance, the return to sketching does not imply simple paper sketching, but rather digitally empowered sketching and drawing. The *digitally enhanced* sketching points also to curious intra-digital developments. Thus, going back to the verbal, to primary designs, to one-scalar thinking (versus multi-scalar design), to sketching and electronic pens slows down the work and makes designers rethink their working techniques and bespoke attachments to nonhumans that make their practice *different*. As the everyday office infrastructures – the face-to-face interactions, the tools and the materials – are central to design work, it is therefore not surprising that the changes to these material conditions related to the pandemic deeply affected the process of architectural practice. They modified the culture of designing architects. They allowed designers to inhabit the world of practice *differently*. New reflexivity on the material and technological conditions of practice emerged.

Stepping aside and speeding up: Technological developments

A lot has been written about how the Covid-19 pandemic prompted the advancement of architectural technologies and IT developments and accelerated the adoption of digital technologies in many fields by several years (McKinsey 2020). In architecture, there has been a marked increase in the use of advanced technologies and the accelerated migration of data into the cloud. Some of these technologies were there before the pandemic but their importance has increased now. The Covid-19 crisis has been a tipping point for technology adoption and digital disruption of major proportions for the architectural and the built environment sector introducing, or mobilizing, some changes that were there since the first (1990s) and the second 'digital turn' (2000s). During those turns, some digital technologies remained dormant and not fully applied at the level of practice due to various organizational and technology issues: that is the required changes represented a shock to the established ways of working in different firms, IT infrastructure was insufficient or organizational silos impeded the execution of the required changes. Thus, architectural practices either failed to prioritize these developments in the past or feared that resistance to change would be a barrier. The pandemic provided an impetus for these developments. Yet, the acceleration of technological processes during the pandemic did not happen in a miraculous way. Architects first stepped aside and began exploring and implementing architectural and IT tools. Digital technologies gained a great deal of importance for practices that had not fully implemented them before or were not ready for them yet, and in particular, the technologies of collaborative working across different industries and geographies. In addition, to facilitate the process of remote design work, more tools for online meeting platforms were developed. Using more digital tools for online working, collective brainstorming, and thinking and drawing together prompted an intra-digital development. We can hardly describe it as another 'digital turn', as some critics have hastily labelled this process.

The first technological challenge in the pandemic was to find the right technology to replace the face-to-face meetings in design reviews commonly conducted in the presence of printed materials where feedback would be communicated in the form of sketches and annotations. Buttress in Manchester shared the change in their work:

> During the pandemic, proposals are shown through the screen share facility on Teams and BIM models are presented using visualisation software. *Feedback is provided by utilising the ProCreate app on an iPad, which allows the design review's facilitator to live sketch onto the presented proposals through the sharing screen on Teams.* Screenshots of the annotated proposals are then captured alongside formal written feedback which is shared among the meeting's participants and saved onto the practice's server.[48]

Adopting new ways of working allowed architects to continue doing design reviews remotely, yet far from the immediacy of paper

FIGURE 3.7 *Face-to-face meeting with clients in the office at Shing & Partners Design Group in Guangzhou, China,* © *Shing & Partners Design Group.*

and human contact. The instant feedback on the work commonly expressed in the form of sketch, annotation or verbal comment is now delayed, more thoroughly formulated and expressed as formal written feedback, shared and saved alongside the presented proposal. Although this technique often alters the nature of feedback, it still allows the practice to ensure that their collaborative culture is retained despite the changing circumstances, and thus ensures a consistent design quality of their work.

Thanks to the pandemic, the Chinese practice Shing & Partners (Figure 3.7) began using BIM software:

> Although BIM has been promoted over a decade ago in China, it wasn't broadly applied until the year of 2020, for its coordination character provides a synergetic working platform for architects and engineers from different disciplines. *Shing & Partners historically completed two projects last year with BIM tools used through the whole process.*[49]

Promoting the use of existing digital tools like BIM to be mobilized now according to their full potential is inevitably changing the way practices operate. It is important to remind ourselves that BIM has been known in the field of architecture for a while. The concept of BIM has existed since the 1970s. The term 'Building Information Model' first appeared in 1992 and became popularly used ten years later. From 2002 to 2003, it has been used in architectural practices as a software facilitating exchange and for interoperability of information in digital format. To the drafting AutoCAD tools, BIM adds further information (time, cost, manufacturers' details, sustainability and maintenance information) to the building model. It is also associated with the second digital turn (Carpo 2013). If the first turn is associated with the shift from mechanical to digital technologies as a major historical turning point in the profession in the 1990s and focused on tools for form finding and mass customization, tools for making, the second shift focused on tools for thinking. BIM is one of them. The years 2000–1 saw a wave of technological tools for prediction, information retrieval and organization associated with the second digital turn. The shift from form-making to process prompted the adoption of new software for information exchange and for the management of building and construction tasks; this family of software, known under the generic name of BIM, has been taking on increasingly important design roles alone. What is significant for BIM is participatory authorship as BIM facilitates the exchange of digitized information among the many agents – human and technical alike – that must interact in large design and construction projects. Thus, in a typical cultural-technical feedback loop, just as 'post-modern culture was the "favourable environment" where digital technologies took root and to which they adapted to finally evolve in the way they did' (Carpo 2013: 10) at the time of the first digital turn, the pandemic culture prompts architectural technologies that facilitate interoperability of action to flourish. Practitioners from different parts of the world began using tools for thinking and coordination (and for discussion, negotiation, feedback, decision-making and storytelling) much more actively which resulted in considerable changes in their working and organizational methods.

In other practices in other parts of the world, the pandemic accelerated the use of web-based project management tools. Architects from the Brazilian practice Sotero Arquitetos account for this development: 'Until March 2020, when the pandemic reached Brazil, our firm's projects were managed via Excel spreadsheets on which we recorded all the phases of each project, listing their duration, who was in charge, client's info, among others.'⁵⁰ The project manager used to follow up and check delivery dates, terms and assigned tasks and deadlines to the team members, updating the sheets by hand. The team itself however did not have access to the control sheets as they used to have their tasks and timelines assigned by their project manager. During the pandemic, when working from home became the 'new normal', architects from this practice realized that they needed a web-based project management tool so that every team could access it readily and some degree of automation could be bestowed upon the operation. They introduced, into their firm, the Asana project management software, which they custom-tailored for their practice. Asana is a tool that allows web-based project management. This resulted in a more efficient control of the tasks performed by the teams working remotely. The app allowed them to improve the planning phase of their projects through the creation of routines and predefined task lists with deadlines, which can be visualized by both the manager and the person assigned the task. Every team could access it readily and this resulted in more efficient control of the tasks and improved the planning phase of projects. As a new 'actor' in the practice Asana began mediating the relationships between the manager and the team members. It improved project coordination and work efficiency. Reflecting on this development, architects state:

> Most of the changes and innovations for us came from adopting or updating software for all tasks. That is, digital technology has gained a great deal of importance in our structure. Project management is now being done entirely remotely without any loss in productivity from our team, even though we saw it as a challenge for not being ready for rapid change. [. . .] We realized that *many of the changes we implemented could have been part of our routine for quite some time*. But the truth is that the need for a quick reaction to the problems brought by the pandemic made all this transformation happen very fast. That being said, we can no longer go back to our old ways. All change is welcome and has been incorporated to our routine successfully.⁵¹

Just like BIM has been in the realm of practice since 2001, Asana has been known since 2008, and the implementation of these tools in practice could have been done much earlier. The pandemic activated some dormant developments. The new tools for collaborative design, project management and communication all triggered little changes in the working routines that redefined the working equilibrium of each practice.

Communication became an important concern for practices. For a big firm like KPMB in Toronto, this year, argue the architects, they 'have employed and deployed every imaginable way *to be in communication – to keep the tribe together*'[52] while also maintaining the distinctive culture of the practice and the cultural coherency that they consider their 'hallmark'. The Chinese practice NODE Architecture & Urbanism with fifteen to twenty designers coming from different parts of China and whose main office is located in Shenzhen also discusses how technological developments were made to 'keep the tribe together':

> As you know, Tencent is a Shenzhen-based, pioneering IT company. During Covid-19, Tencent has launched the Tencent Meeting App, which is efficient and easy to work with, and has quickly become a very useful tool among Chinese users' groups. I don't see online working or meetings in Shenzhen as being much different from the rest of the world. Perhaps even more so, *Shenzhen has adapted to the new situation with the state-of-art online technology easily and more quickly than any other city*.[53]

In addition to fostering new IT developments and communication apps, like Tencent, the pandemic also prompted digital processes and other IT developments that were under construction in some practices for some time. Reflecting on these developments, architects from the Israeli practice HQ Architects in Tel Aviv state:

> Architecture is a field of work where changes don't happen overnight. Things are meant to take time, yet the recent and ongoing pandemic proved that change can be a fast process especially in the working environment, and in this case, in the architectural profession as a whole. For us at HQ Architects the pandemic brought the challenge as well as the opportunity *to enhance and update our connectivity and upgrade technological infrastructure* to meet deadlines, clients' and contractors' expectations and maintain the quality of our work in the office

and on construction sites. The pandemic had a huge impact on ways of communication in the office, *affecting the way we work and coordinate as well as the office culture and day to day life*.[54]

The practice put great effort and care in upgrading their digital systems to facilitate the team's remote work and invested in their digital presence. They bought laptops for the entire team to ensure that everyone can work efficiently from home and provided staff with the resources to continue working. They also implemented cloud-based infrastructure:

> We saw the opportunity to take a huge leap forward and we went on the cloud. By providing cloud-based infrastructure we improved the quality, efficiency and safety of information passed through, providing an efficient, flexible and collaborative working environment for all. *Digital tools helped us communicate better with our collaborators overseas, where Zoom calls were the norm even before the pandemic, now we became savvier.* Using digital tools such as Zoom and GoToMeeting, we continued our participation in architecture talks, conferences and summits, connecting with our peers and audiences internationally when boarding on a plane was neither safe nor possible.[55]

Thus, by upgrading and investing in their digital presence, HQ Architects ensured they could respond to the pandemic challenges without missing 'any opportunities that arise'. While, undoubtedly, prior to the pandemic architectural practices were already adopting and adapting various types of digital tools, from design to project management, the pandemic had accelerated many processes that were already under consideration in practices. It *prompted* architects to search for digital tools that would respond to their needs and implement them to speed up processes that were embryonic. All these developments triggered small variations in working practice, daily routines and office culture.

Similar to HQ Architects in Tel Aviv, quite a few practices – for example, Philippe Rahm Architects in Paris, Buromoscow in Moscow, Architecture for Humans in Kosovo, and others – have already established routines for 'trans-local working' across time zones. Husos architects from Madrid have always operated online in a transnational way. For instance, between 2003 and 2005, while working on the 'Host and Nectar Garden Building', they were already using MSN Messenger intensively as a medium through which to carry out project management during the construction of the building, between Madrid, where the firm is based and Cali, Colombia where the project happened. MSN Messenger was the most common platform at the time that helped the office operate in a transnational way. The pandemic made them go back to this way of working. This time they had to gather 'the dispersed office' across several places – Cyprus, Canada, Spain and Belgium – as they worked on a small project, 'A Moulting Flat'. Construction took place in 2020 and took longer than the usual time due to Covid-19 restrictions. Reflecting on how this experience differed from previous years, they state: 'Besides working from the microscale, our office operated trans-locally, however – this time dictated by a sense of immediacy and thus, differently to our previous experiences.'[56]

Other small practices that had operated remotely pre-Covid-19 also witnessed changes:

> Luckily, since a large part of our team works from abroad, we were quite comfortable working from a distance, which is something that most likely many architectural practices have experienced in the last few years [. . .]. With all the bad that this pandemic has brought on us, it has also shown that *certain parts of our work need rethinking*, especially since the building industry is still one of the last ones to be drastically improved because of ICT and technology.[57]

This need of rethinking technologies and to constantly keep up with the improvements in ICT and digital technologies in all sectors of the built environment is shared by many practices. Technologies that have been there for a while now, due to the pandemic, entered architectural practices and stirred positive developments.

Yet, if smaller practices engaged in rethinking their working methods, implementing new technologies and project management tools to enhance their working methods, for the larger practices, the pandemic accelerated the process of pulling resources from different branches of a practice together. Offices of the same firm distributed across geographies became closer as daily and weekly catchups with the studio teams became the norm.

One of the biggest changes is that w*e are no longer defined by our ·geography and office location* which encourages greater collaboration between staff from all studios, ensuring that the skills and knowledge required for each project can be more focused. The remote working has enabled the pool of resources to be widened beyond the constraints of the individual studios, and staff are supporting one another more as a collective. This has also enabled all staff to have a greater awareness of more projects within the practice. The daily routine starts with the management team catch-up which is an opportunity to establish where peaks and troughs in workload are and identify where resource support is needed. This has embedded a more collective responsibility to meet all deadlines and to support each other in achieving the overall goals of the practice. This is something that we have been trying to establish for some time, but the last year has ensured that this has become embedded in the practice.[58]

Thus, escaping geographic definition and limits, the improved communication increased the quality of design work for practices like Seven Architecture. The more connected the branches of this big practice became, the more resourceful the use of office expertise got, and the more architects became aware of other projects within the firm (Figure 3.8). This resulted in a strong sense of collective responsibility and ownership for the firm's projects. Although Seven Architecture had started implementing the use of Microsoft Teams previously, it has now become the normal practice and has been an essential tool in hosting internal and external meetings, updating projects and keeping staff up to date, discussing financial performance and initiatives for improving health and well-being. Like in other practices implementing BIM, Asana or new cloud infrastructure, the firm Seven Architecture has been trying to implement Teams for some time but has succeeded to embed it in the everyday routines of the practice only now during the pandemic.

Land+Civilization Compositions is based across three locations, Hong Kong, Shenzhen and Rotterdam, and they need technologies to communicate on a daily basis.

What Covid has done is *to allow the reality of our work to emerge*. We are a dispersed team that collaborates. There is not such a clear hierarchy. *The digital tools that were always there*

FIGURE 3.8 *Work at the firm 'Seven Architecture', Manchester and Harrogate, UK, © Seven Architecture.*

> the last 10 years had to be leveraged – but enabled and exposed an inherent truth. At least in our work, it is not the work of a singular author. And speaking to the reality of the work beyond the bounds of 'our office', Covid has *blurred what is the edge of our office and that of the client, builder, collaborators*. It is more of a blurry blob of us working together now to generate spaces and places.[59]

Listening to Jason Hilgefort from Land+Civilization Compositions, we can argue that the introduction during the pandemic of digital tools and technologies that were in the field for some time, has played as a major 'breaching experiment' on its own. Now that the pandemic accelerated their implementation and allowed practices to use them to their maximum potential and to the maximum advantage of architectural firms, a dormant reality was revealed. One that we all saw but said little about – the fluid webs of design making lead to diluting all hierarchical structures. The technologies introduced a new redistribution of forces and had a 'flattening' effect on practices by dissolving traditional hierarchies and established roles, blurring even the clear boundaries between clients, builders, collaborators and architects and highlighting, even more, the collective effort and cooperative dynamics of architecture-making. This echoes the argument by the Brazilian practice arquiteto paisagista, discussed earlier, for whom each video call flattens the roles but also the physicality of the participants. The 'background expectancies' of designers revealed in the 'breaching experiment' set by the newly introduced technologies were to find and reinstate flatness at each phase of a design project. In fact, that is how design work is ordinarily created and maintained, and that is how designers organize their acting together, not in fixed hierarchies and strictly defined roles. All pandemic technological developments highlighted, even more, the fluid and versatile character of design making.

Thus, stepping aside, looking around and repopulating the practice with old or new tools and apps of collaborative design, project management and communication, that is tools for thinking and action, architects began rethinking their working methods during the pandemic. More and more digital tools piled up causing intra-digital developments. The tools introduced and deployed triggered *little differences, minimal actions* and *small variations* that redefined the working ecology of each practice and allowed them to inhabit the world of design in a different way.

New compositions: Reconnecting with the 'others'

Instead of choosing between the physical and the digital Zoom world, architects have engaged in inventing new hybrid ways of communicating with clients and collaborators. Designers from the Hassell Studio in London described how the pandemic affected their work on a major project for a campus redevelopment at the American University in Cairo (AUC). The firm had been commissioned to develop the Learning Space Strategic Plan for AUC, to create a rich landscape of settings for learning and to enrich both on campus and remote learning by reusing and adapting spaces, buildings and landscapes that would better suit their future needs. Before the pandemic, they had undertaken an extensive analysis across the whole campus and had begun discussions with various faculties, academics and students. Hosting intensive on-site workshops to map spaces that were working well, they planned what could be improved and identified as opportunities for intervention into the existing campus. Six months into the project, the pandemic began and greatly affected their way of working:

> Due to the pandemic, we were then hit hard by the lack of face-to-face time due to Covid-19 restrictions. Culturally Egyptians are open, friendly, hospitable and natural team players and face-to-face communication was really important to them. We were as a result of the restrictions challenged in *how to communicate the considerable level of detail in our work* and remote working exacerbated this issue.
>
> We, therefore, had to switch completely to using Zoom and Teams for meetings, workshops and presentations, and a number of challenges were faced. This included the international aspect of the work being in London, Chicago (a key project partner was located there) and Cairo. So, we had three time zones to negotiate. In addition, we had to manage differing levels of Covid responses in different countries as they worked through their actions and responses to the pandemic. This had an impact on how and when we could meet virtually, the location of our team members and access to technology [. . .]. In particular, we had to adapt our way of working in terms of stakeholder consultation and workshops which in the past we would have led in a face-to-face environment. This was no longer possible due to travel restrictions. *For AUC, this was particularly challenging due to their cultural context and expected ways of working.*[60]

Julian Gitsham, principal at Hassell Studio in London and his team, were required, then, to come up with creative ways of conducting group engagement from a distance via Zoom. For instance, they had used pre-prepared slides whereupon the participants could use the annotation function in Zoom to draw arrows, write notes and respond with emojis. In Zoom discussions and digital workshops, architects from Hassel Studio discussed with academics and students about their working practices, what changes they could foresee, and analysed their typical activities on campus. Then they discussed the ideal characteristics for the spaces needed to support those different activities and reviewed the ideal settings that would enable their best work based on individual spaces, collaborative spaces and shared spaces. At the completion of each activity, the groups were asked to discuss their thoughts and ideas, and these were marked up and annotated on screen remotely. This feedback was important 'to build an understanding of the client's reaction'[61] and the chat facility created an opportunity for the clients to contribute directly. Conversely, 'the opportunity for attendees to have a voice through chat facility opened up much more widely the chance for others to contribute, to be listened to and heard in this new way of working'.[62] With a project of that scale and complexity and for 'the Learning Space Strategic Plan' to work as a comprehensive campus-wide piece of work, it was critical that the architects absorb significant details from the client's perspective. That is why the communication of information and clients' concerns via the remote working methods had to be managed in an extremely careful way.

The changing rapport with clients is reported by other practices as well. KPMB in Toronto, for instance,

> found *a new availability of clients*. The fact that senior leaders in all fields are also in lockdown has created a level of accessibility that means they are available to discuss, answer questions, and engage in collaborative decision-making. I called the CEO and the Senior Director on my projects to make sure they knew what we were doing and to share thoughts with them individually and 'in person' with cameras on. They too have struggled with the communication challenge and sharing ideas and information has been a major benefit. In the first months of the pandemic I called people directly, particularly those who had hired our firm as part of a competitive interview process, and with whom there had been direct interaction. Some were surprised and seemed pleased that I had reached out, and all extended our conversations broadly. The *contact was welcomed and set up a new level of relationship that went beyond the confines of the project and extended to sharing strategies for leadership during unprecedented and unanticipated times.*[63]

While big firms like KPMB invest any effort in rethinking and re-designing the modalities of relations with their clients, benefiting from their new availability, and connecting with them in new ways and at different levels, in another context, in Sydney, Australia, architects from the firm Fake Industries engage in reinventing the relations with local communities. The practice has projects, partners, clients and collaborators from different geographical locations. The low incidence rates in Australia in 2020 also curtailed Covid-19's impact on their daily routines. The city was in full lockdown for only a few weeks in the Autumn of 2020, and the use of masks was never fully implemented. In contrast, travel restrictions, rigorously implemented in Australia at a national and regional level, required them to adapt the way that they do things. Overseas meetings were cancelled or transferred to online platforms. These changes were 'more disruptive for clients who often wish to meet the architect in person'[64] than to the architects' working routines.

During the pandemic Urtzi Grau, principal of Fake Industries, and his team were working in Murrin Bridge on a project for an Aboriginal community in New South Wales, which includes an extension of the local Preschool and Community Hub. Working for the Aboriginal community involved extensive consultation processes, participatory workshops and close communication with various institutions, agencies, community leaders, service providers and the general public that shares an interest in the project. When travel restrictions in Australia prevented them from travelling within New South Wales to meet their clients and the community that they were designing for, architects were forced to think quickly about possible solutions:

> Completing these activities online proved challenging as clients wish to meet the architect in person. For example, *the preschool kids' response to a face on the screen is different from in-person interaction. Working with Aboriginal communities in Australia requires building and maintaining trust*, and Zoom's corporate environment does not help.
>
> We resorted to *surrogates* to complete the consultation and participatory processes while the regional lockdown was in place. We worked with collaborators already in the area who facilitated the workshops and even impersonated us. We prepared in advance for online meetings with our local representatives and became stage directors, giving directions for a play that would happen later in the week. *The sessions were strange and exciting, as we witnessed through a screen someone else doing our job*, talking to the preschool students and their teachers or explaining

the project to the Aboriginal Land Council. As much as we wanted to intervene, *our voice coming out of a laptop could not compete with the physical presence of our surrogate*. The inevitable lost in translation made these workshops different, opened them up to unforeseen insights on the project.⁶⁵

'Designing' *surrogates* of architects is a resourceful hybrid arrangement indeed (Figure 3.9). Not only did architects treated the sanitary measures as a design problem and began restructuring and reorganizing office spaces, as seen in many practices mentioned earlier, extending the design to devise online digital proxies of the missed physical spaces, of those special sites for social and informal exchange, but also, they designed their own human replicas, finding and identifying suitable collaborators in the area, preparing and briefing them on the project, and most importantly, training them how to act and talk like architects. What a wide remit of architectural expertise, reaching so far as to include techniques for

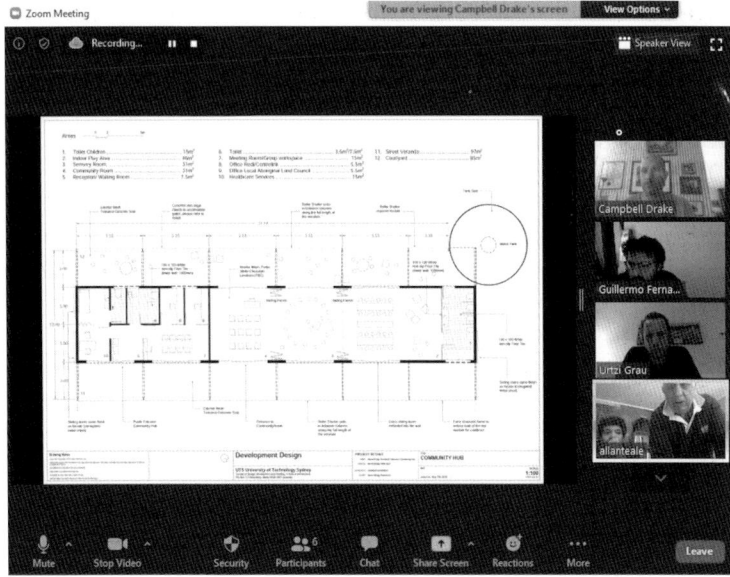

FIGURE 3.9 *Meeting with communities and the architect's surrogate,* © Fake Industries.

staging the designer's own presence in community meetings. Instead of hiding behind Zoom, architects have become stage designers and directors at the same time, giving instructions for a strange play. This hybrid method allowed them to maintain a remote authority by 'designing' their own presence while taking a different role by supervising the entire process through Zoom and witnessing the clients and users enjoy the physical presence of their surrogate on site. This also introduced an interesting criticality from within – witnessing 'someone else doing your job from a distance' provides further reflexivity on the job.

These new 'tactics' of collecting feedback from the clients (Hassell Studio), reconnecting with clients in new ways (KPMB) and fabricating designers' surrogates to connect with local communities (Fake Industries) introduced new compositions of forces (Foucault 1995) in practice to make it work as an efficient machine during the pandemic reminiscent to the *dispositifs* we have witnessed in urban space (Chapter 2). By employing these new 'tactics', the architectural practices introduced new coded activities and trained aptitudes in clients and communities of users, crafting new and different combinations of creative forces, and prescribing new ways of doing things.

Another hybrid composition emerges from the work of Berlin-based practice Brenne Architects. They are currently overseeing the renovation of a Renaissance chateau; a project that had begun in 2019, and over the course of 2020 and 2021 was in its design phase. The condition of the building had been meticulously recorded and examined in detail, and architects are currently working on specific aspects, like the renovation of the historic heating system, its barrier-free access and the design concept for the interior rooms that are to be used for events, among others. While meetings with clients would have normally taken place in the client's administrative offices at a table with a rolled-out plan, in the light of the Covid-19 restrictions, they are held online. Whereas meetings used to take place in weekly or bi-weekly 'jourfixes', especially for large projects, now there are fixed recurring appointments on Zoom for the various meeting groups. Online meetings may save travel time and are shorter in length, important decisions nevertheless require more time, more discussion and several rounds of consultations. It is therefore difficult to take those decisions online:

Planning documents are prepared which will be discussed in detail at meetings with project managers from the client, our staff and, depending on the topic, other specialist planners are being present. Since the building is over 300m long and the work involves the entire building, the discussion of the plan online via Zoom is particularly tedious. Since the plan can never be displayed in its entirety on the computer without losing the readability of details – the constant zooming in and out poses a particular hurdle – we have therefore started to hold planning meetings on site, but outdoors with masks.

Last week, for example, we met on site to discuss the sealing applications in the basement (Figure 3.10). *This meeting would normally have taken place in the client's administrative offices at a table with a rolled-out plan, but because of Covid, it has now become an on-site visit.* We always meet at the main entrance to say hello and then go to the areas that need to be discussed. So last week we had to discuss the procedure for waterproofing

FIGURE 3.10 *Hybrid meeting of the team of Brenne Architects at the Orangery Palace,* © *Brenne Architects.*

the basement. Five of us, this time with the restorer and the conservationist, went into the cellar and walked from room to room looking at the walls and floors and discussing damp damage. The plans we had brought with us, extracts in A3 so that they are handy, were placed on the floor, but it was too dark in the cellar, so in the end we gathered standing around an opened laptop to explain and discuss the waterproofing plan. It was a speedy meeting that allowed decisions to be made on the spot about the type of waterproofing. *The building and its materiality, specific damage and, in this case, the height of the basement rooms, which delay the rise of moisture to the wooden surface on the ground floor, are all present in this decision-making process.* Much more present than before in meetings on paper.[66]

Instead of relying on the building physicist's survey, expert opinion and working out the planning solutions on this basis, Fabian Brenne and his team rely on the building's capacity to communicate its 'needs'. Holding planning meetings on site, close to the building areas that need discussion and intervention, walking around, inspecting the damages, interacting with the building, architects attempt to devise better solutions. The plans (present either as extracts in A3 placed on the floor or on the computer) are consulted and compared to visible traces in the building. This composite setting allows decisions to be made on the spot and enables the building to be literally 'present' in the room, instead of being represented by the survey. Its materiality interferes directly with decision-making processes. As a result, special techniques were invented for bringing the building 'in the room of discussions'.

Another hybrid response was devised by l'atelier d'architecture autogérée (aaa) in Paris. This is a participatory practice that involves working with communities in suburban neighbourhoods in Paris led by Doina Petrescu and Constantin Petcou. In the context of their participatory practice, Doina and Constantin were required to organize 'meetings with people who are not digitally literate or simply do not have access to digital equipment for online meetings, under the conditions of imposed cap on the number of persons in a room and travel restrictions'. These meetings took place in relation to the activities of two R-Urban hubs called Agrocité Gennevilliers and Agrocité Bagneux which had continued to function during the pandemic. The R-Urban network devised by the practice addresses communities from urban and suburban contexts, which typically involve a range of participants – residents, local authorities, public organizations, professionals and civic stakeholders – who take various responsibilities in the projects' governance. The two hubs specialize in urban agriculture and are managed by local residents who live in social housing estates in different suburban cities in the Parisian region. They host 'civic resilience' practices that include recycling, food growing, energy production, among others. Due to the limit on the number of people that can be in a room and the travel restrictions architects form aaa invented a new way of organizing these meetings with residents:

> Since March 2020, we have started to organize 'hybrid' meetings (Figure 3.11a, 3.11b), combining online presence and presence on site involving a limited number of people (more recently only

FIGURE 3.11A *Hybrid meeting of the architects from l'atelier d'architecture autogérée with communities at Agrocité Bagneux, March 2021, © l'atelier d'architecture autogérée.*

FIGURE 3.11B *Agrocité Bagneux, March 2021, © l'atelier d'architecture autogérée.*

up to six). During these meetings, one member of our team was in change to provide the digital infrastructure. This involved a mobile computer with access to an online video conferencing platform (in our case it was meet-coop, as we want to support an alternative platform which corresponds to the socio-ecological approach we promote through R-Urban). *The format was quite successful as it maintained a minimal collective presence on site while there were restrictions on travel and public space occupancy. We also helped the users to make video reportages to be shared on social media.* We were able to support the connections amongst users and to maintain a continual contact with the site for those who were not able to be there.[67]

This was an important occasion for the hubs to demonstrate their role in supporting civic resilience in challenging times, praised also by the French newspaper *Le Parisien* for providing 'bubbles of fresh air and [. . .] solidarity' (Bureau and Riou 2020) in the heart of social housing estates. It offered an opportunity for the architects to make an impact on these vulnerable communities affected by the pandemic. If Hassel Studio and Fake Industries were concerned with reinventing ways to reconnect with the client and the communities of users, devising new tactics for integrating clients' feedback, communicating complex details and understanding their reactions despite the cultural difference as well as staging the architect's presence in client meetings, aaa had engaged in rethinking the connectivity with others by maintaining a form of hybrid communication, a mixture of face-to-face and Zoom meetings to ensure a level of inclusivity.

Being concerned with 'others', not just the clients but those 'others' whose lives are affected by the work of architects, aaa architects assume an important ethical role in the creation of empowering spatial relationships, which are also social. They act as interpreters while also accepting uncertainty as an inescapable feature of their practice. In these cases, whether in Cairo, Murrin Bridge, Toronto or the Parisian *banlieue*, architects work from within the intricate contexts of particular communication issues with clients and communities rather than observing them from the outside, that is, from the comfort of their respective offices in London, Sydney, Toronto or Paris. By doing so, they relish an engagement with contingency and act as interpretative agents, as powerful stage designers of new resourceful choreographies of communication. It is one of those rare occasions, when 'Architecture's dependency (from the others), far from being its weakness, becomes its opportunity, with the architect acting as an open-minded listener and fleet-footed interpreter, collaborating in the realization of other people's unpolished visions' (Till 2009: 164). Crafting also, we should add, the spaces, the compositions, the surrogates and the dispositions that would afford possibilities for these visions to be expressed, shared, understood and realized. None of the solutions offered by these practices were directly expressed in the design of an object, a building or a master plan. Instead, architects channelled their efforts in evaluating and making sense of complex situations, looking forward to and negotiating new sets of social relations, of compositions of forces and entire new *dispositifs,* to be able to exercise a transformative agency.

Curiously, in some firms, this hybridization of practice continues as architects have returned to face-to-face meetings, and some online techniques, protocols, conventions and digital tricks are further adapted to the offline modus operandi of many practices. Architects from Atelier TeamMinus in Beijing 'believe that the face-to-face discussion can give us the most inspirational atmosphere' and during the pandemic, most of the meetings with clients were held in the face-to-face regime. Yet, they developed many new online ways of brainstorming to refresh their ordinary work patterns. Reflecting on this change, they elaborate: 'now, while our work is almost back to normal, we still sometimes apply this Zoom annotation + Wacom mode in the offline meeting.'[68] They also invite their clients to draw their own ideas on digital 3D models since this method proved to be an easily accessible way for clients to engage with the design and ensured a smooth process of communication during the lockdown. This mode of 'offline meeting with online tools' proves to be an efficient bridge between the hand-sketch-based work process and the dynamic digital architectural expression. Currently, many offline meetings follow methods developed with online tools, and more newly established ways of working are transferred back to physical space as architects engage in reinventing these spaces with the digital in mind.

Tele-working and digital communication have resulted for some in the reshuffling of geographical distance and the erosion of time zones. Most architects valued the possibility of working in different locations, both home and office, in and from different countries. Being able to work remotely, one architect explains, 'I [can] now divide my time and work between an established Italian office and a young German firm.'[69] For the French firm Philippe Rahm Architects, 'there are not really time zones anymore. I found myself in appointments at 2 am on Zoom because I was in Taiwan, and I had to be in Switzerland in the afternoon.'[70] For them, for better or worse, tele-work generates 'a continuous space and time, without the old respite of the night and the private home'.[71] Working between Moscow and Hong Kong to design in Havana, architects from Buromoscow, recount their endless 'zooms' while 'moving' across geographies: 'today the vastness of Moscow suburbs, the snowfall, the cold, the greyness, the old cars in improvised garages, the prefabricated housing blocs, the security guards, the concrete Lachman fences, the barbed wire, the deserted rail tracks – all of it fills the zoom screen and enters their bright and warm Hong Kong afternoon. Bringing the worlds together.'[72] For architects from K&K

in Thessaloniki, 'changing virtual rooms, meetings with potential partners, connecting from one zoom "room" to another' creates the illusion of displacement, of movement in space, a routine so much missed by everyone. 'It strangely feels like literally walking from one meeting to another.'[73] For other firms, working in the pandemic felt like being part of a perpetuum mobile of design, taking day-and-night shifts. Designers from NODE Architecture & Urbanism in Shenzhen were joined in 2020 by a US team to participate in a design competition in Shenzhen. They share: 'for the first round of the "idea competition", our joint work was not really affected by the pandemic. On the contrary, because of the time difference, two teams worked in the manner of day-and-night shifts, which turned out to be quite an efficient way to team up and work.'[74] 'Longer nights, shorter days, like Ramadan': that is how Firas Sweidan from the Urban Planning Center remembers work in lockdown. 'Last year during Ramadan, most of the meetings and coordination had to be scheduled between 9.00 pm and 2.00 am as most people (even the clients) slept more in the mornings and stayed up longer at night for Suhour, and the magical word became: "do you have your computer"!'[75] Before Covid-19, architects from this Jordanian practice used to work for nine hours a day, sometimes extra hours were involved depending on the projects. Now, due to the curfew, they are working longer hours since they have their computers at home, and it is becoming harder to stop working especially when there are pressing deadlines.

There is no doubt that the pandemic accelerated the perpetuum mobile of the design venture. Yet, instead of falling into the illusion of the disappearance of geographical distance and time zones or the 'illusion of displacement, of movement *in* space', a different consistency of relations in practice was instated. Architectural practitioners became more realistic and their activities have gained a depth that was not possible before. Rethinking, repopulating and resituating their practices, their descriptions in the ethnographic responses have made visible what their practice truly depends on, what they are attached to, what they engage with and what has implications for them. Each practice offered a unique and concrete composition of new forces. The fluidity, the disturbing dematerialization of space and time that risks creating a floating reality and evaporation of presence, ceases to be a danger when we witness the specific adjustments of practices on the ground.

Innovation in practice

Paying specific attention to the texture of the daily work of architects in a period of crisis by highlighting the local, situated and embedded nature of architectural knowledge, we have reflected on various examples of pandemic variations of practice that offered opportunities to witness how architects across the globe continue to develop their craft. This little experiment with architectural firms has shown that practitioners engaged in slowing down, going back and rethinking, stepping aside and speeding up, and designing new compositions, exploring the implications and the entanglements of practice. A special choreography indeed. As the pandemic unfolded, architectural firms crafted new practical adjustments in the rhythm and formats of design making. The ordinary working habits of practices were 'breached', and the tacit beliefs and rules became visible. New relational dynamics between architects, clients and communities of users emerged, reshuffling traditional patterns of teamwork, hierarchies, expertise and communication tactics, nudging them even to 'design' their own surrogates and to 'bring' the building into meetings. By introducing this transformative movement, Covid-19 acted as an element of metamorphosis, triggering a complex, fragmented and overflowing movement, changing the state of things in architecture, shaping new material, spatial and technological *dispositifs* of practice. And yet, it is important to remember that there has been no big revolution, no radical new 'turn', but a movement that gradually introduces these little differences, these minimal actions. Felt as a shudder, each of these changes makes the stability of the practices tremble, and eventually regain equilibrium.

The practitioners' responses have shifted scholarly attention towards the local circumstances of production of architectural knowledge, the material culture, the spatial arrangements and technologies that impact the current conditions of practice. At the level of design practice, there are no big discourses or manifestos, but a nebula of small changes and tiny variations – returns, positions, displacements, reintroductions and rediscoveries. A myriad of small beings – online communication apps, old and newly discovered digital tools for design or project coordination, digitally enhanced pens, storytelling, writing and narrative tactics, surrogates of architects and clients, among others – populate architectural studios around the world. It is this diversity of beings and practices that is at the basis of the invention and at the same time forms its outcome. Pandemic practices, therefore, can only be described and understood as composed of these small actions (Tarde 1999b) rather than gathered around professional identities, solidarities, ethics and values. Similar to Garfinkel who used the breaching experiment to make a point in the 'professional politics' of sociology, our study demonstrates the need to pay close attention to the dynamics of design innovation rather than explain it with the conventional categories offered by sociologists of the profession (social, economic and political factors). Whether in Shenzhen or Wellington, Moscow or Montréal, Amman or Buenos Aires, what brings practitioners together are not different regulations, Accreditation Boards, Plans of Work or codes of professional conduct that in spite of their national specificity all have the common aim of providing stability for the profession, but rather that very *movement* of rethinking the ecology of their design practice.

Instead of explaining the small variations of practice with the big changes that the pandemic has introduced, of fitting the details within larger frames, emphasis was placed on the overall similarities between architectural firms in distant contexts and between the accumulations of elementary actions and minimal changes they introduced in their work. Thus, the big pandemic change can be gradually understood by tracing the small inventions, and the radical shudder triggered by Covid-19 with the small adjustments in design practice. There were no existing solutions to the challenges that architectural practices faced during the pandemic. The course of repetitive design work generated a continuous production of small innovations and adjustments that circulated and provided solutions. When repeated and imitated by the same practice and then by others, these inventions propagated and accumulated, often leading to bigger differences; the cycle starts again. This is the fundamental rhythm, the *basso continuo*, that can offer a realistic understanding of design practice in pandemic times. Only by tracing the multiplicity of individual innovations produced in practice, can the effects of the pandemic and how their accumulation will mingle together in a post-Covid-19 era be fully accounted for. Through small movements and imitations, these inventions can spread, and through them, the pandemic society can gradually change.

In addition, our enquiry into the modalities of pandemic design practice has illustrated the amazing potential of architecture to reinvent itself. More than ever, architects appeared not just as detached polishers of form and shapes but as resourceful agents that gather conflicting voices and concerns, make sense of complex situations and devise technological and materially smart suggestions that could have wider social impact. No big revolutionary heroes, indeed, but efficient agents, 'good craftsmen' that work on the ground within constraints and contingency. Operating across different scales, mobilizing wider networks of practice, pandemic designers have relied on experimentation, turning the difficulties and the restrictions imposed by the pandemic into opportunities, accepting the incompleteness and the precarity of the adjustments crafted with designerly means. As paradoxical as it might sound, these pragmatic arrangements at a time of social distancing have generated hope for reinventing the spatial dynamics of social relations.

Conclusion

Architectural research extended to things

Filling space with swarming and din, the parasite is an expansion; it runs and grows. It invades and occupies. It overflows, all of a sudden, from these pages. Inundation, swelling waters.

(SERRES 1982: 253)

As the invisible coronavirus killer marched through across the globe, causing major disruptions over the past year or so, we began to rethink the conditions through which to design cities, practice and study architecture. Causing unprecedented spatial expansion, Covid-19 had phenomenally changed cities and the work of urban practitioners. In this book, I offered a chronicle of several key transformations that range from the spatial lab-like architecture of pandemic cities to the 'laboratories' of architecture-making.

First, I discussed the new spatial choreography of daily life and the radical laboratorization of urban space. Describing and analysing some key variations in pandemic cities, I reflected critically on the specific ways the virus transformed typologies and gradually changed the spatial choreography of daily life turning city dwellers into subjects and participants in experiments. Different tactics and protocols from the lab and the field of medical diagnosis began playing a role in spatial architecture. In order to capture the virus, in order to spot it and detect the various forms it takes – in urban space, in buildings but also in technology, in different rituals and practices – special lab-like *dispositifs* were erected; while capturing the virus, subjects were also turned into objects and metamorphosed. Tracing the changes in urban space and the different variations of the laboratorized city, we also witnessed how the social link was redefined by the Covid-19 virus to include numerous nonhumans (sanitizers, dividers, temperature robots, floor markers and pictograms). New materials and machines populated our cities as Perspex and plastic replaced concrete and wood, albeit, perhaps, only temporarily. The prevailing pandemic technologies of disease prevention, traceability, visibility and distance regulation slowly and gradually began transforming contemporary architecture, turning buildings into porous and flexible *mega-dispositifs* of capture. Regulating curves of visibility, distances, signals, objects and streams of floating contactless bodies, they actively promoted the dissolution of the boundaries of architecture, of the structure that contains, and defied all static understandings of space and built form. As design played an active role in regulating flows of movements, calibrating distances, impeding touch and dispatching energies, a new architectural sensitivity resurfaced. Straying away from concerns of aesthetics and functionality, the key design choices oriented around considerations on how to prevent and minimize physical surface contact, and thus a new 'modulor' emerged, one that turned around the scale of the touch. Humans became hunters and victims of entrapment – handless, strolling, floating, *traceable*, but hardly containable and fully controllable.

Multiplying through to its smallness and occupying space with imperceptibility, the coronavirus, we argued here, acted through metamorphosis. The affected flows of the city started circulating more quickly. The city reacted. The flows accelerated and the defensive system was mobilized. The virus introduced a transforming movement of life itself, an improbable, complex, fragmented, bursting movement, dancing like a wall of fire. Yet, it did not radically transform the city as such, but simply changed its energetic state. It shifted the city around minimal angles and diagonals. Far from inducing a revolution, a radical change, Covid-19 triggered little differences, minimal actions and differential changes of state. These minuscule differences do not allow us to predict big transformations or foresee their specific character. No more than a shudder, the virus made cities tremble, paradoxically, to ensure their stability. If the small effects of its intrusion, displacements and fluctuations are well tolerated, the virus could reinforce the city's resistance and increase its adaptability; potentially a new equilibrium can be established.

Second, drawing on ethnographic responses of 130 architectural practices from around the globe, I discussed the new innovations, material adjustments and new epistemic habits in practice that have emerged in response to pandemic restrictions. Yet, architectural firms were not reduced, at any moment, to a mere microcosmic index of the macrocosmic social and economic transformations during the pandemic. The analysis of the inventions in practice and new modalities of knowledge production in architectural design offered an invitation to engage pragmatically with the ongoing changes and provided glimpses into aspects of the pandemic architectural practice around the world. Architects from different places opened the doors of their houses and offices and shared mundane stories of struggle, adventure and resourcefulness, agreeably showing those special practical adaptations that helped them to survive. The different *dispositifs* of pandemic practice accounted for by practitioners illustrated how the virus transmogrified the way designers communicate, act, discuss, brainstorm, experience materials, draw, learn about a building and enact their own presence, and through these small transformations, a metamorphosis in design practice was traced. They allowed us to witness the impact of the global pandemic on the wider ecology of architectural practice, but also to trace, conversely, how numerous small metamorphoses at the level of design practice have led gradually and cumulatively to larger social and cultural effects. The little changes in practice have steered the reshuffling of roles and responsibilities in design firms, freeing designers from rigid and burdensome hierarchies, unlocking the hidden potential of the youngest, turning the makers into writers, the shy into vocal, the underrepresented into visible. More trust was delegated to architects with unconventional ideas and attitudes to risk-taking. In addition, as the gap between thinkers and makers got diluted, the boundaries between the designers' and clients' offices became more blurred, reshaping further the team dynamics and the broader social ecology of work.

Historicity and virus

Moving around, making noise and occupying space, the new coronavirus made history. And it is this recent history that I unravelled, a history written or told as a network of bifurcations where viruses alike move about. But how is history made? And what is history? Traditionally, we consider history as the possibility of distinguishing between a 'before' and an 'after', the creation of irreversible situations, of winners and losers; doctrines are dismissed, theories are overturned; there is no possible return to a previous situation as we have all moved on. A steady and irreversible linear course becomes evident from the past to the present, that industrious arrow of time.

Yet, there is a different understanding of history as *historicity*. This term refers not just to the steady passage of time – that the seventeenth century follows the sixteenth century, or that 2022 follows 2021, which, in turn, follows 2020 – the death of adversaries, the dismissal of doctrines, a new era, but to the fact that *something happens in time*, that history not only passes but also transforms, that it is made not only of dates but also of events, of mediations – like the virus – that resist being flattened out onto a linear timeline. The bifurcated history of 2020 and 2021 accounted here has really shown how *events* confuse the idea that time follows a line.

Over the past months, as we have tried to make sense of the irruption of Covid-19 into our lives, when we could no longer imagine a time before or foresee a time after, we witnessed how coronavirus made history by becoming an *event* and made implausible the conventional philosophy of history in which an object remains immobile, inactive or ahistorical. The concept of *event* (a term borrowed from the philosopher Alfred North Whitehead) explains better novelty and replaces the notion of discovery, turn, revolution and radical change. Foregrounding the notion of event has consequences for the historicity of all the ingredients of history, including nonhumans. Following closely how the events unfolded in the city as we followed arrows and read new pictograms and as we changed habits and routines, we can argue that it is impossible to understand what coronavirus really did to us, to our cities and to architectural design without detecting, tracing and accounting carefully for the heterogeneous network of transformations as they happened. The virus emerged and became apparent amid all these urban metamorphoses and small changes in architectural practice; due to these changes, it has a life, a history of its own.

And if history has often served humans, these recent events convinced us that things can have history, and things can make history. The important historical 'agent' – Covid-19 – is not mentioned in this book in any metaphorical or ironic sense, but rather becomes a pragmatic reality outliving its semiotic definition. There is no definite list of factors that could explain what happened in the past few months. Unravelling the small transformation in cities, the pervasive presence of lab-like *dispositifs* in urban space and buildings, the uncertainties, agitations and passions surrounding the virus, allows us to tell a story of how it makes history, not by moving from past to present, but from one type of intertwining to an even bigger intertwining, a bigger inter-connectivity, a larger entanglement of innovation techniques.

The pandemic went everywhere as the virus multiplied, and that is the logic of every pandemic. But more importantly, it affected all relations. The position of each virus is to be in between, an arrow that intercepts. An operator, something that interrupts from the middle, a relation of relations. Because of its unprecedented spread, this novel coronavirus attacked more massively, more aggressively, the relations than the beings. Becoming a mediator in many relations, just like any parasi 1982) it took the place of the third: the third between the client and the architect, between the user communities and the designers' surrogates; interrupting their dialogue, adding noise onto their messages. In a way, the virus intervened to re-establish what was not preestablished in practices and buildings. It did so, also, to facilitate the relations, to sometimes optimize them, to sometimes simplify them. This intervention, however, complicated the city and the creative apparatuses of architectural practices. It led to new branching lab-like settings that, in turn, parasitized on cities and buildings. Distributively included in all relations, intercepting all of them between all the locations, capturing all the flows, the coronavirus as an included third, began re-establishing relations both in cities and in practices, by intervening. Invading space and time, the virus grew. It is now everywhere.

New reflexivity, new methods

Meanwhile, a new reflexivity among practitioners has emerged. Here are some of the prominent voices:

Voice 1:

> The pandemic has served to justify errors, changes and delays. It has become a scapegoat. It has justified more than mobility problems, industry closures or medical illnesses. Whether they were real or exploited causes, *the pandemic has fostered a more understanding environment*. It has allowed negotiations to be more open and creative in seeking solutions to the problems that occurred. These attitudes could be summarized in that all the agents have had greater empathy and have had a more elastic thinking.[1]

Voice 2:

> The comfort and functions of the basic living contents are compressed on a pragmatic level in architecture, functional units and contents in public buildings also require *new ways of designing and thinking about space*, which consequently changes architecture as a discipline, i.e. what was traditionally considered necessary now faces a new challenge of redefining both private and public spaces.[2]

Voice 3:

> However, we have witnessed a slight increase in interest by the public and contractors for our innovative apartment designs (e.g. the concepts elaborated around '*Do you really want to live like your mother?*', the 'Elastic Apartment', 'Slim City' and others). Many of our concepts, built or not, are now being used and appreciated without reservation.[3]

Voice 4:

> Many private customers in the design market start to slow down the pace of development and pay *more attention to the quality*

of the design rather than the speed. For small design firms like ours pursuing creativity and quality, there are more challenges but also more opportunities.[4]

Voice 5:

> As the relationship between health and inequality has been so manifest by the pandemic and has risen on the public agenda, so has our commitment to ensure we practice ethically. As a direct consequence of Covid-19 we have become more politicised and more outspoken in drawing attention to how the built environment reproduces inequities in social relations. We aim to make plain our intent *to serve the communities that will occupy our work, so that social equity is embedded in everything we attempt to achieve.*[5]

Voice 6:

> I believe that Covid brought up not only the necessity of keeping high health and safety standards on sites, but especially in Greece where *many workers come from foreign, low-income countries, it brought up the issue of the lack of correct training and education in personal health protection* in crews employed in medium or small projects.[6]

Thus, with the slowing down, close attention to quality and creativity was paid, leading to a greater understanding, empathy and openness (Langarita Navarro architects, Madrid), a new thinking about space (STONE DESIGN, Skopje) related to more 'elastic' ways of living (PPAG architects, Vienna and Berlin) and more attention to 'the quality of design' (11ARCHITECTURE, Shenzhen). At the same time, a new social awareness emerged (Sarah Wigglesworth Architects, London) when new ethical and social dimensions of practice were raised, and issues of labour and equity were addressed (2Jarchitects, Athens). These trends highlighted by the practitioners also echo some of the key themes in the semantic map of the architectural debate (Figure I.1) and resonate with the main societal discussions that the global pandemic has sparked. Yet, the map can hardly offer insights into the concrete challenges experienced by designers at the level of architectural practice. Nor can it wholly capture the concerns of the city dwellers, the clients or the planners. To fully understand the current challenges, we cannot rely on one method only. The map allows us to shift to bigger constructs, in which the concrete pandemic realities of designing architects undergo a process of deliberate reduction and abstraction. While distant readings of the map enable us to see broader trends, a closer ethnographic lens, where specific voices can be heard, offers insights into particular pandemic adjustments in practice. A dialogue between the mapping and specific situations captured ethnographically can facilitate a movement from the extraordinary to the every day, from a large mass of facts to exceptional single events at the level of the practice, from a macrohistorical to a microhistorical treatment of architecture, and back.

Therefore, architectural theorists and historians should be the first to rethink qualitative research methods at a time of social distancing just as architects are the first to rethink the new spatial choreographies of the post-pandemic city. Exploring complex and unfolding changes in architectural practice requires us to mobilize both close and distant methods and can inevitably trigger a new and unprecedented cross-fertilization between architecture and other fields. The pandemic prompts us to invent hybrid formats of enquiry that can replace actual contact and immersed observation, not with their obvious digital equivalents (close with distant, qualitative with quantitative), but with a skilfully crafted network of investigatory tactics that engage in subtle recalibrations of distances, combine further close and distant, and intensify the depth of the enquiry.

The combination of these readings can signal new directions for both the theory and history of architecture. Interesting questions of method emerge: What kind of history is possible with quantitative tools? Can the historiography of the present be based on a 'close digging' into the current conditions of a present that will lend itself more easily to 'distant reading'? How is the manoeuvring between close and distant methods different than canonical historical or anthropological readings? And if, these methods are combined, complementing each other, can quantitative and qualitative data in tandem generate better anthropology-informed historiography of the present? These are all big questions for such a short duration of eighteen or twenty months while the onerous task of good historians is to cover years, decades and centuries. Yet, the epistemic gain is not to be measured by the extent of the periods covered, but rather by the ability of these composite methods to make sense of the complex underlying dynamics in practice. This requires us to rethink the perennial relationship between and the reciprocal relevance of macrohistory and microhistory of architecture, and to address the fundamental epistemological problem, raised by Paul Ricoeur (2004), of how to aggregate data. What is noticeable with distant readings (on maps and graphs) is difficult to grasp with ethnographic experiments, what can be extracted from the grain of specific anthropological situations can hardly be seen on digital maps. After all, capturing dynamics in small- and medium-size firms, rather than just big-star architects' practices, will contribute to a more inclusive approach to practice. It will also promote *a pragmatist approach to history writing*. One that is based on concrete and small actions, actors' statements, witnessing unfolding design variations and urban metamorphoses, rather than established discourses, sedimented in various archives, after the dust has settled down.

As all these changes in cities, in practice and in the field of architectural theory and history continue to unfold in myriad profound but unpredictable directions, it is now the right time to turn this virus into a cause for thinking and rethinking our cities, our practices and our disciplines. This would mean learning to design in such a way that collective thinking will proceed in the presence of viruses and sick bodies who would otherwise likely be disqualified. That is to think in a way that listens to 'a democracy that can only be conceived if it can freely traverse the now dismantled border between science and politics, in order to add a series of new voices to the discussion, voices that have been inaudible up to now, although their clamour pretended to override all debate: the voices of nonhumans' (Latour 2004: 69). There are millions of subtle mechanisms capable of adding new voices to this chorus that can be further intensified by design. Just as the social and spatial conditions of pandemic life still in flux are enticing architects to craft new adjustments, it is up to us, to devise our own methodological adjustments so as to be able to capture all those often-unaccounted voices in the chorus, new and old, distant and close, individual and aggregated, subtle and distinct, modest and loud.

Although my ambition here is not to speculate on possible scenarios for the future of practice or reflect on the long-term implications of this crisis on architecture, questions about the architectural practice in a post-Covid-19 era will remain. What would it mean to practice architecture after the pandemic? What technologies and materials will prevail? Who will gain power in shaping post-pandemic cities? How will designers account for the complex scenarios of social connectivity and social distancing in future planning? How will the pandemic formats of practice prepare us for design in a post-pandemic era? Some possible answers are lurking behind the 'thick descriptions' and methodological experiments provided in this book. Yet, it is up to you to address them, not through speculations, but through new resourceful adjustments in practice.

NOTES

Introduction

1 Ethnographic response, Sarah Wigglesworth, Sarah Wigglesworth Architects, London, UK, 9 March 2021.

Chapter 3

1 Zoom interview with Nicola Russi, Laboratorio Permanente, Milan, Italy, 29 June 2020.
2 Ibid.
3 Ethnographic response, José Humberto Gómez Architecture, Caracas, Venezuela, 11 March 2021.
4 Zoom interview with Paola Gatti, Negozio Blu Architetti Associat, Torino, Italy, 30 June 2020.
5 Zoom interview with Paolo Dellapiana, Dellapiana ARCHICURA, Turin, Italy, 29 June 2020.
6 Ethnographic response, Nicola Gurrieri, Ahochdrei – Labor für Gestaltung / Studio Gurrieri Associati, Berlin, Germany and Florence, Italy, 16 March 2021.
7 Ethnographic response, Konrad Buhagiar, Konrad Buhagiar Architects, Birkirkara, Malta.
8 Zoom interview with Paolo Dellapiana, Dellapiana ARCHICURA, Turin, Italy, 29 June 2020.
9 Zoom interview with Gustavo Ambrosini, Negozio Blu Architetti Associati, Turin, Italy, 30 June 2020.
10 Ethnographic response, José Humberto Gómez Architecture, Caracas, Venezuela, 11 March 2021.
11 Ethnographic respones, Julian Dickens, Dickens Architects, London, UK, 11 October 2021.
12 Ethnographic questionnaire, Achim Kaufer, ac.ka architects, Berlin, Germany, 15 March 2021.

13 Ethnographic response, Bostjan Vuga, Sadar+Vuga, Ljubljana, Slovenia, 17 February 2021.
14 Ethnographic response, Kevin Daly, kdA, Los Angeles, USA, 19 March 2021.
15 Ethnographic response, Firas Sweidan, Urban Planning Center, Amman, Jordan, 14 March 2021.
16 Ethnographic response, Anna Popelka and Georg Poduschka, PPAG architects, Vienna, Austria and Berlin, Germany, 26 March 2021.
17 Ethnographic response, John McLaughlin, John McLaughlin Architects, Dun Laoghaire, Ireland, 31 March 2021.
18 Ethnographic response, Ljupco Tasevski, Stojan Pavleski, Ivan Simeonov and Gjorgi Radovanovic, STONE DESIGN, Skopje, Republic of North Macedonia, 11 March 2021.
19 Ethnographic response, Eric Shing from Shing & Partners Design Group, Guangzhou, China, 15 March 2021.
20 Zoom interview, Marco Pippione and Giovanni Durbiano, DAR, Turin, Italy, 15 June 2020.
21 Ethnographic questionnaire, Jan Kasl, JK ARCHITEKTI s.r.o., Prague, The Czech Republic, 23 March 2021.
22 Ethnographic response, Simon Saint, Woods Bagot, London, UK, 20 March 2021.
23 Ethnographic response, María Langarita and Víctor Navarro, Langarita Navarro, Madrid, Spain, 15 March 2021.
24 Ethnographic response, Rena Sakellaridou, RS SPARCH, Athens, Greece, 13 March 2021.
25 Ethnographic questionnaire, Firas Sweidan Jordan, Urban Planning Center, Amman, Jordan, 14 March 2021.
26 Ethnographic response, Duarte Vaz, arquiteto paisagista, Rio de Janeiro, Brazil, 19 March 2021.
27 Ibid.
28 Ethnographic response, Diego Arraigada, Diego Arraigada Arquitectos, Rosario, Argentina 16 March 2021.
29 Ibid.
30 Ibid.
31 Ethnographic response, Dr Dana Cuff, Director, cityLAB – UCLA, Los Angeles, USA, 13 March 2021.
32 Ethnographic response, Marcelo Carvalho Ferraz, Brasil Arquitetura Studio, São Paulo, Brazil, 26 February 2021.
33 Ibid.
34 Questionnaire, Simona Della Rocca, BDR bureau, Turin, Italy, 23 April 2020.
35 Zoom interview with Gustavo Ambrosini, Negozio Blu Architetti Associati, Turin, Italy, 30 June 2020.

NOTES

36 Zoom interview with Nicola Russi, Laboratorio Permanente, Milan, Italy, 29 June 2020.
37 Ethnographic response, Jason Hilgefort, Land+Civilization Compositions, Hong Kong/Shenzhen/Rotterdam, 15 March 2021.
38 Ethnographic response, Diego Barajas & Camilo García, Husos architects, Madrid, Spain, 16 March 2021.
39 Zoom Interview with Marco Pippione, DAR, Turin, Italy, 23 August 2020.
40 Ethnographic response, Diego Barajas & Camilo García, Husos architects, Madrid, Spain, 16 March 2021.
41 Ethnographic response, Ljupco Tasevski, Stojan Pavleski, Ivan Simeonov and Gjorgi Radovanovic, STONE DESIGN, Skopje, Republic of North Macedonia, 11 March 2021.
42 Ethnographic response, Rasha Samawi, Architectural Division | CC GROUP, Amman, Jordan, 14 March 2021.
43 Ibid.
44 Ethnographic response, Huishu Deng, Atelier TeamMinus, Beijing, China, 14 March 2021.
45 Ethnographic response, Mark Foster Gage, Mark Foster Gage Architects, NYC, USA, 19 February 2021.
46 Ethnographic response, Nick Mouat, Athfield Architects, Wellington, New Zealand, 15 March 2021.
47 Zoom interview with Dana Cuff, Los Angeles, USA, 14 October 2020.
48 Ethnographic response, Gavin Sorby, Managing Director, Buttress, Manchester, UK, 12 March 2021.
49 Ethnographic response, Eric Shing from Shing & Partners Design Group, Guangzhou, China, 15 March 2021.
50 Ethnographic response, Adriano Rapassi Mascarenhas, Sotero Arquitetos, Salvador, Brazil, 15 March 2021.
51 Ibid.
52 Ethnographic response, Marianne McKenna, KPMB, Toronto, Canada, 26 February 2021.
53 Ethnographic questionnaire, Doreen Heng LIU, NODE Architecture & Urbanism, Shenzhen, China, 15 March 2021.
54 Ethnographic response, Erez Ella, HQ Architects, Tel Aviv, Israel, 11 March 2021.
55 Ibid.
56 Ethnographic response, Diego Barajas & Camilo García, Husos architects, Madrid, Spain, 16 March 2021.
57 Ethnographic response, Rron Beqiri, Architecture for Humans, Prishtina, Kosovo, 15 March 2021.
58 Ethnographic response, Lisa McFarlane, Seven Architecture, Manchester and Harrogate, UK, 15 March 2021.

59 Ethnographic response, Jason Hilgefort, Land+Civilization Compositions, Hong Kong/Shenzhen/Rotterdam, 15 March 2021.
60 Ethnographic response, Julian Gitsham, Principal, Hassell Studio, London, UK, 23 March 2021.
61 Ibid.
62 Ibid.
63 Ethnographic response, Marianne McKenna, KPMB, Toronto, Canada, 26 February 2021.
64 Ethnographic response, Urtzi Grau, Fake Industries, Sydney, Australia, 10 March 2021.
65 Ibid.
66 Ethnographic response, Fabian Brenne, Brenne Architekten GmbH, Berlin, Germany, 15 March 2021.
67 Ethnographic response, Doina Petrescu, Constantin Petcou, Atelier d'Architecture Autogeree, Paris, France, 28 March 2021.
68 Ethnographic response, Huishu Deng, Atelier TeamMinus, Beijing, China, 14 March 2021.
69 Ethnographic response, Nicola Gurrieri, Ahochdrei – Labor für Gestaltung // Studio Gurrieri Associati, Berlin, Germany and Florence, Italy, 16 March 2021.
70 Ethnographic response Philippe Rahm, Philippe Rahm Architects, Paris, France, 22 February 2021.
71 Ibid.
72 Ethnographic response, Olga Aleksakova, Buromoscow, Moscow, Russia, 19 March 2021.
73 Ethnographic response, Katerina Kotzia, Korina Filoxenidou, K&K Architects, Thessaloniki, Greece, 15 March 2021.
74 Ethnographic questionnaire, Doreen Heng LIU, NODE Architecture & Urbanism, Shenzhen, China, 15 March 2021.
75 Ethnographic response, Firas Sweidan, Urban Planning Center, Amman, Jordan, 14 March 2021.

Conclusion

1 Ethnographic response, María Langarita and Víctor Navarro, Langarita Navarro, Madrid, Spain, 15 March 2021.
2 Ethnographic response, Ljupco Tasevski, Stojan Pavleski, Ivan Simeonov and Gjorgi Radovanovic, STONE DESIGN, Skopje, Republic of North Macedonia, 11 March 2021.
3 Ethnographic response, Anna Popelka and Georg Poduschka, PPAG architects, Vienna, Austria and Berlin, Germany, 26 March 2021.

4 Ethnographic response, Jing Xie, 11ARCHITECTURE, Shenzhen, China, 16 March 2021.
5 Ethnographic response, Sarah Wigglesworth, Sarah Wigglesworth Architects, London, UK, 9 March 2021.
6 Ethnographic response, Souaila Tzagnoun-Kotaki, 2Jarchitects, Athens, Greece, 2 March 2021.

BIBLIOGRAPHY

Abbas, M., 'Can Public Transportation Survive the Pandemic? Experts Warn of "Death Spiral"', *NBC News*, 27 December 2021. Available online: https://www.nbcnews.com/tech/tech-news/can-public-transportation-survive-pandemic-experts-warn-death-spiral-n1252214 (accessed 17 January 2021).

Adams, B., Marenko, B. and Traganou, J., eds, 'Design in the Pandemic: Dispatches from the Early Months', *Design and Culture*, 13, no. 1 (2021): 1–8.

Alexander, C., Ishikawa, S. and Silverstienm, M., *A Pattern Language: Towns, Buildings, Construction*, New York: Oxford University Press, 1977.

Baldwin, A. N., 'SARS and the Built Environment in Hong Kong', *Municipal Engineer*, 159, no. 1 (2006): 37–42.

Barlow, N., 'Plans Could See The Whole of Deansgate Turned Into a Car Free Zone', *About Manchester*, 2020. Available online: https://aboutmanchester.co.uk/plans-could-see-the-whole-of-deansgate-turned-into-a-car-free-zone/ (accessed 18 January 2021).

Bird, J., Kriticos, S. and Tsivanidis, N., 'Impact of COVID-19 on Public Transport', *IGC*, 2020. Available online: https://www.theigc.org/blog/impact-of-COVID-19-on-public-transport/ (accessed 15 January 2021).

Boeri, S., *Urbania*, Roma: Editori Laterza, 2021.

Bollack, F., *Old Buildings, New Forms: New Directions in Architectural Transformations*, NYC: The Monacelli Press, 2013.

Brand, S., *How Buildings Learn: What Happens after They're Built*, New York: Viking, 1994.

Brown, N., Buse, C., Lewis, A., Martinand, D. and Nettleton, S., 'Air Care: An "Aerography" of Breath, Buildings and Bugs in the Cystic Fibrosis Clinic', *Sociology of Health & Illness*, 42, no. 5 (2020): 972–86.

Brown, P., 'CAD: Do Computers Aid the Design Process After All?', *Intersect: The Stanford Journal of Science, Technology and Society*, 2, no. 1 (2009): 52–66.

Bruegmann, R., 'La representation architecturale et l'ordinateur: Du crayon à la table à dessin électroique', in E. Blau and E. Kaufman (eds), *L'architecture et son image: Quatre siècles de representation architecturale*, 138–55, Montréal: Centre canadien d'architecture, Éditions du Méridien, 1989.

Bureau, O. and Riou, A., 'A Bagneux et Gennevilliers, les Agrocités, bulles d'air et de vert pendant le confinement', *Le Parisien*, 13 November 2020. Available online: https://www.leparisien.fr/hauts-de-seine-92/a-bagneux-et-gennevilliers-les-agrocite-bulles-d-air-et-de-vert-pendant-le-confinement-13-11-2020-8408255.php (accessed 26 March 2021).

Burge, P., 'Sick Building Syndrome', *Occupational and Environmental Medicine*, 61, no. 2 (2004): 185–90.

Callon, M., 'Le travail de la conception en architecture', *Situations Les Cahiers de la recherche architecturale*, 37 (1996): 25–35.

Carpo, M., *The Digital Turn in Architecture 1992–2012*, London: John Wiley and sons, 2013.

Cirrincione, L., Plescia, F., Ledda, C., Rapisarda, V., Martorana, D., Moldovan, R. E. and Cannizzaro, E., 'COVID-19 Pandemic: Prevention and Protection Measures to be Adopted at the Workplace', *Sustainability*, 12, no. 9 (2020): 3603.

Colomina, B., *X-Ray Architecture*, Zurich: Lars Müller, 2019.

Construction+, 'MiC Technology Applied in Pak Heung Temporary Quarantine Facilities', *constructionplusasia.com*, 29 May 2020. Available online: https://www.constructionplusasia.com/hk/pak-heung-temporary-quarantine-facilities/ (accessed 24 June 2021).

Corsin Jimenez, A., 'Anthropological Entrapments: Ethnographic Analysis Before and After Relations and Comparisons', *Social Analysis: The International Journal of Anthropology*, 65, no. 3 (2021): 110–30.

Cucinotta, D. and Vanelli, M., 'WHO Declares COVID-19 a Pandemic', *Acta Biomed*, 91, no. 1 (2020): 1.

Cuff, D., *Architecture: The Story of Practice*, Cambridge, MA: MIT Press, 1992.

Cuff, D., Loukaitou-Sideris, A., Presner, T., Zubiaurre, M. and Crisman, J., *Urban Humanities: New Practices for Reimagining the City*, Cambridge, MA: MIT Press, 2020.

Culbertson, A. and Aguilar-Garcia, C. (2021), 'Coronavirus: Why Public Transport Could Be Safer Than We Thought', *Sky News*, 7 October 2020. Available online: https://news.sky.com/story/coronavirus-why-public-transport-couldbe-safer-than-we-thought-12091657 (accessed 18 January 2021).

Da Silva, D. C., King, D. A. and Lemar, S., 'Accessibility in Practice: 20-Minute City as a Sustainability Planning Goal', *Sustainability*, 12 (2020): 129.

Deleuze, G., 'What is a Dispositif ?' in T. Armstrong (trans.), *Michel Foucault, Philosopher: Essays*, 159–66, New York: Harvester Wheatsheaf, 1992.

Deleuze, G., *Cinema 2: The Time-Image*, London: Athlone Press, 1989.
Dierig, S., Lachmund, J. and Mendelsohn, A., eds, 'Science and the City', *Osiris*, 18 (2003).
Domínguez, D., Beaulieu, A., Estalella, A., Gómez, E., Schnettler, B. and Read, R., eds, 'Virtual Ethnography', *Forum Qualitative Sozialforschung / Forum: Qualitative Social Research*, 8, no. 3 (2007): 1–4.
Farías, I. (2015), 'Epistemic Dissonance: Reconfiguring Valuation in Architectural Practice', in A. Berthoin Antal, M. Hutter and D. Stark (eds), *Moments of Valuation: Exploring Sites of Dissonance*, 271–89, Oxford: Oxford Scholarship Online.
Farías, I. and Wilkie, A., eds, *Studio Studies: Operations, Topologies and Displacements*, New York: Routledge, 2016.
Fisk, W., Mirer, A. and Mendell, M., 'Quantitative Relationship of Sick Building Syndrome Symptoms with Ventilation Rates', *Indoor Air Journal*, 19, no. 2 (2009): 159–65.
Forgan, S., 'The Architecture of Science and the Idea of a University', *Studies in History and Philosophy of Science Part A*, 20, no. 4 (1989): 405–34.
Forty, A., 'The Modern Hospital in England and France: The Social and Medical Uses of Architecture', in A. D. King (ed.), *Buildings and Society: Essays on the Social Development of the Built Environment*, 32–50, London: Routledge, 1980.
Forty, A., *Words and Buildings: A Vocabulary of Modern Architecture*, New York: Thames & Hudson, 2004.
Foucault, M., 'The Confession of the Flesh', in C. Gordon (ed.), *Power/Knowledge Selected Interviews and Other Writings*, 194–228, New York: Pantheon Books, 1980.
Foucault, M., *Discipline and Punish*, New York: Vintage Books, 1995.
Furet, F., 'Quantitative History', *Daedalus*, 100, no. 1 (1971): 151–67.
Galison, P., *Image and Logic: A Material Culture of Microphysics*, Chicago: University of Chicago Press, 1997.
Galison, P. and Thompson, E., eds, *The Architecture of Science*, Cambridge, MA: The MIT Press, 1999.
Garfinkel, H., *Studies in Ethnomethodology*. USA: Polity Press, 1991.
Gell, A., 'Vogel's Net: Traps as Artworks and Artworks as Traps', *Journal of Material Culture*, 1, no. 1 (1996): 15–38.
Gell, A., *Art and Agency*, Oxford: Oxford University Press, 1998.
Gieryn, T., 'Biotechnology's Private Parts (and Some Public Ones)', in A. Thackray (ed.), *Private Science*, 219–53, Philadelphia: University of Pennsylvania Press, 1998.
Gieryn, T., 'Two Faces on Science: Building Identities for Molecular Biology and Biotechnology', in P. Galison and E. Thompson (eds), *The Architecture of Science*, 423–59, Cambridge, MA: MIT Press, 1999.

Gieryn, T., 'City as Truth-Spot: Laboratories and Field-sites in Urban Studies', *Social Studies of Science*, 36, no. 1 (2006): 5–38.

Gooday, G., 'The Premises of Premises: Spatial Issues in the Historical Construction of Laboratory Credibility', in J. Agar and C. Smith (eds), *Making Space for Science: Territorial Themes in the Shaping of Knowledge*, 216–45, Basingstoke: Palgrave Macmillan, 1998.

Gottschling, P., 'To Submit is to Relate: A Study of Architectural Competitions within Networks of Practice', PhD diss., The University of Manchester, Manchester, UK, 2016.

Hine, C., *Virtual Ethnography*, London: Sage, 2000.

Holmes, D. and Marcus, G., 'Collaboration Today and the Re-Imagination of the Classic Scene of Fieldwork Encounter', *Collaborative Anthropologies*, 1, no. 1 (2008): 81–101.

Horve, P., Lloyd, S., Mhuireach, G., Dietz, L., Fretz, M., MacCrone, G. and Ishaq, S., 'Building Upon Current Knowledge and Techniques of Indoor Microbiology to Construct the Next Era of Theory into Microorganisms, Health, and the Built Environment', *Journal of Exposure Science & Environmental Epidemiology*, 30 (2020): 219–35.

Hosseini, M., Fouladi-Fard, R. and Aali, R., 'COVID-19 Pandemic and Sick Building Syndrome', *Indoor and Built Environment*, 29, no. 8 (2020): 1181–3.

Houdart, S. and Chihiro, M., *Kuma Kengo: An Unconventional Monograph*, Paris: Éditions Donner Lieu, 2009.

Isso, J. (2021), 'Schumer: More Than $4 Billion For MTA Included In COVID-19 Stimulus Deal', *Ny1.com*, 20 December 2020. Available online: https://www.ny1.com/nyc/all-boroughs/transit/2020/12/20/COVID-19-stimulus-deal-new-york-city (accessed 17 January 2021).

Jacobs, J. and Merriman, P., 'Practising Architecture', *Social & Cultural Geography*, 12, no. 3 (2011): 211–22.

Jafari, M. J., Khajevandi, A. A., Mousavi Najarkola, S. A., Yekaninejad, M. S., Pourhoseingholi, M. A., Omidi, L. and Kalantary, S., 'Association of Sick Building Syndrome with Indoor Air Parameters', *Tanaffos*, 14, no. 1 (2015): 55–62.

James, Frank A. J. L., ed., *The Development of the Laboratory: Essays on the Place of Experiment in Industrial Civilization*, London: Macmillan Press, 1989.

Jenkins, L., 'Geography and Architecture: 11, Rue du Consevatoire and the Permeability of Buildings', *Space and Culture*, 5, no. 3 (2002): 222–36.

Kaji-O'Grady, S. and Smith, C. L., *LabOratory: Speaking of Science and its Architecture*, Cambridge MA: MIT Press, 2019.

Klonk, C., ed., *New Laboratories: Historical and Critical Perspectives on Contemporary Developments*, Berlin: De Gruyter, 2016.

Knorr-Cetina, K., *The Manufacture of Knowledge*, Oxford: Pergamon, 1981.

Kulper, A. C., Crouse, K. and Liese, J., eds, *Portals: Pedagogy, Practice, and Architecture's Future Imaginary (RISD 2020)*, Barcelona: Actar, 2021.

Latour, B., 'Give Me a Laboratory and I Will Raise the World', in K. Knorr-Cetina and M. Mulkay (eds), *Science Observed: Perspectives on the Social Study of Science*, 141–71, Los Angeles: Sage, 1983.

Latour, B., *Science in Action: How to Follow Scientists and Engineers Through Society*, Cambridge, MA: Harvard University Press, 1987.

Latour, B., *The Pasteurization of France*, trans. A. Sheridan and J. Law, Cambridge, MA: Harvard University Press, 1988.

Latour, B., *Jubiler ou les difficultés de l'énonciation religieuse*, Paris: La Découverte, 2002.

Latour, B., *Politics of Nature: How to Bring the Sciences into Democracy*, Cambridge, MA: Harvard University Press, 2004.

Latour, B., 'What Protective Measures Can You Think of So We Don't Go Back to the Pre-crisis Production Model?' *AOC*, 29 March 2020. Available online: https://aoc.media/opinion/2020/03/29/imaginer- les-g estes-barrieres-contre-le-retoura-la-production-davant-crise/ (accessed 15 November 2020).

Latour, B., *After Lockdown: A Metamorphosis*, London: Wiley, 2021.

Latour, B. and Woolgar, S., *Laboratory Life: The Social Construction of Scientific Facts*, Beverly Hills: Sage Publications, 1979.

Latour, B. and Yaneva, A., 'Give Me a Gun and I Will Make All Buildings Move: An ANT's View of Architecture', in R. Geiser (ed.), *Explorations in Architecture: Teaching, Design, Research*, 80–9, Basel: Birkhäuser, 2008.

Lebahar, J. C., *Le dessin d'architecte: simulation graphique et reduction d'incertitude*, Marseille: Parenthèses, 1983.

Le Corbusier, *Le Modulor: Essai sur une mesure harmonique à l'échelle humaine, applicable universellement à l'architecture et à la mécanique*, Boulogne: Éditions de l'Architecture, 1950.

Le Corbusier, *Modulor 2: La parole et aux usagers*, Boulogne-Billancourt: Éditions de l'Architecture d'aujourd'hui, 1955.

Lee, S. H., 'The SARS Epidemic in Hong Kong: What Lessons Have We Learned?', *Journal of the Royal Society of Medicine*, 96, no. 8 (2003): 374–8.

Lefebvre, P., '"What the Wood Wants To Do": Pragmatist Speculations on a Response-Able Architectural Practice', *Architectural Theory Review*, 22, no. 1 (2018): 24–41.

Lindner, C. and Sandoval, G. F., *Aesthetics of Gentrification: Seductive Spaces and Exclusive Communities in the Neoliberal City*, Amsterdam: Amsterdam University Press, 2021.

Liu, L., Miller, H. J. and Scheff, J., 'The Impacts of COVID-19 Pandemic on Public Transit Demand in the United States', *PLoS ONE*, 15, no.

11 (2020). Available online: https://doi.org/10.1371/journal.pone.0242476 (accessed 15 March 2021).

Livingston, D., *Putting Science in its Place: Geographies of Scientific Knowledge*, Chicago: Chicago University Press, 2003.

Llach, D. C., *Builders of the Vision: Software and the Imagination of Design*, London: Routledge, 2015.

Loos, A., *Ornament and Crime: Selected Essays*, London: Penguin Classics, 1924.

Lovec, V., Premrov, M. and Žegarac Leskovar, V., 'Is There Any Relation between the Architectural Characteristics of Kindergartens and the Spread of the New Coronavirus in Them? - A Case Study of Slovenia', *Sustainability*, 12, no. 24 (2020). Available online: https://www.mdpi.com/2071-1050/12/24/10363/htm (accessed 1 February 2021).

Ludewig, J. and Leach, A., 'Covid—Quid Tum?', *Architectural Theory Review*, special issue, 24, no. 2 (2020): 182–3.

Lynch, M., *Art and Artifact in Laboratory Science. A Study of Shop Work and Shop Talk in a Research Laboratory*, London: Routledge, 1985.

Lynch, M., *Scientific Practice and Ordinary Action: Ethnomethodology and Social Studies of Science*, Cambridge: Cambridge University Press, 1993.

Lyon-Callo, V., Madra, M., Özselçuk, C., Randall, J., Safri, M., Sato, C. and Boone, W., *Pandemic and the Crisis of Capitalism: A Rethinking Marxism Dossier*, Association for Economic and Social Analysis, Brighton: ReMarxBooks, 2020.

Marcus, G., *Para-Sites: A Casebook against Cynical Reason*, Chicago: University of Chicago Press, 2000.

Mattern, S., 'Purity and Security: Towards A Cultural History of Plexiglass', *Placejournal*, December 2020, Available online: https://placesjournal.org/article/purity-and-security-a-cultural-history-of-plexiglass/?cn-reloaded=1&cn-reloaded=1 (assessed 22 August 2021).

McCullough, M., Mitchell, W. and Purcell, P., eds, *The Electronic Design Studio: Architectural Knowledge and Media in the Computer Age*, Cambridge, MA: MIT Press, 1990.

McKibbin, D., 'How will COVID-19 Change Our Travel Behaviour?', *Research Matters*, 7 March 2020. Available online: https://www.assemblyresearchmatters.org/2020/05/07/how-will-Covid-19-change-our-travel-behaviour/ (accessed 13 February 2021).

McKinsey & Company, 'How COVID-19 Has Pushed Companies over the Technology Tipping Point—and Transformed Business Forever', *McKinsey & Company*, 5 October 2020. Available online: https://www.mckinsey.com/business-functions/strategy-and-corporate-finance/our-insights/how-COVID-19-has-pushed-companies-over-the-technology-tipping-point-and-transformed-business-forever# (accessed 23 April 2021).

McLeod, M., 'Architecture and Politics in the Reagan Era: From Postmodernism to Deconstructivism', *Assemblage*, 8 (1989): 22–59.

Megahed, N. A. and Ghoneim, E. M., 'Antivirus-Built Environment: Lessons Learned from COVID-19 Pandemic', *Sustainable Cities and Society*, 61 (2020): 1–7.

Mommersteeg, B., 'Variations of a Building: An Ontological Politics of Architecture', PhD diss., The University of Manchester, Manchester, 2020.

Moreno, C., Allam, Z., Chabaud, D., Gall, C. and Pratlong, D. (2021), 'Introducing the "15-Minute City": Sustainability, Resilience and Place Identity in Future Post-Pandemic Cities', *Smart Cities*, 4: 93–111.

Moretti, F., *Graphs, Maps, Trees: Abstract Models for Literary History*, London: Verso, 2005.

Murphy, M., *Sick Building Syndrome and the Problem of Uncertainty. Environmental Politics, Technoscience, and Women Workers*, USA: Duke University Press, 2006.

Neurath, O., 'From Vienna Method to ISOTYPE', in M. Neurath and R. S. Cohen (eds), *Empiricism and Sociology*, 220, Reidel: Dordrecht, 1973.

Nickl-Weller, C. and Nickl, H., eds, *Healing Architecture*, Germany: Braun, 2013.

Novoselov, K. and Yaneva, A. (2020), *The New Architecture of Science: Learning from Graphene*, Singapore and NYC: World Scientific Publishing.

Oklahoma State University (2020), 'OSU Researchers Examine Social Distancing Models, Encourage Caution', *Oklahoma State University News and Media*, 7 April. Available online: https://news.okstate.edu/articles/communications/2020/osu-researchers-examine-social-distancing-models-encourage-caution.html?fbclid=IwAR2jgOm81Cn2UL3IEe8XNQEnkzf5zSAv5CqQHnkxQ5CgKH1dFJhRuNxLAg0 (accessed 10 June 2020).

Overman, H. and Nathan, M., 'Will Coronavirus Cause a Big City Exodus?', *LSE Blog*, 10 December 2020. Available online: https://blogs.lse.ac.uk/COVID19/2020/12/10/will-coronavirus-cause-a-big-city-exodus/ (accessed 24 August 2021).

Packham, A., 'The Problem With Perspex: Why Covid Screens Might Not Be Safe. Ministers have Been Told the Screens Should be Scrapped. Here's What the Science Says', *Huffpost*, 17 June 2021. Available online: https://www.huffingtonpost.co.uk/entry/perspex-screens-covid-safe_uk_60ca1846e4b0d2b86a818355 (accessed 5 August 2021).

Passenger Transport, 'We see a Lasting Effect of the COVID-19 Pandemic', *Passenger Transport*, 28 May 2020. Available online: http://www.passengertransport.co.uk/2020/05/we-see-a-lasting-effect-of-the-COVID-19-pandemic/ (accessed 15 June 2021).

Pickering, A., *Science as Practice and Culture*, Chicago: University of Chicago Press, 1992.

Rafalovich, A., 'Making Sociology Relevant: The Assignment and Application of Breaching Experiments', *Teaching Sociology*, 34, no. 2 (2006): 156–63.

Ricoeur, P., *Memory, History, Forgetting*, Chicago: University of Chicago Press, 2004.

Ritzer, G., 'Ethnomethodology', in *Sociological Theory*, 4th edn, 373–99, New York: McGraw-Hill, 1996.

Rogers, B., 'Coronavirus Won't Be the End of Big Cities', *Centre for London*, 27 May 2020. Available online: https://www.centreforlondon.org/blog/the-city-isnt-dead/ (accessed 24 August 2021).

Rose, G., Degen, M. and Melhuish, C., 'Networks, Interfaces and Computer-Generated Images: Learning from Digital Visualisations of Urban Redevelopment Projects', *Environment and Planning D: Society and Space*, 32, no. 3 (2014): 386–403.

Sahlins, M., *Anahulu: The Anthropology of History in the Kingdom of Hawaii, vol. 1, Historical Ethnography*, Chicago: University of Chicago Press, 1992.

Schneider, T., Awan, N. and Till, J., *Spatial Agency: Other Ways of Doing Architecture*, London: Routledge, 2011.

Schön, D., *The Reflective Practitioner: How Professionals Think in Action*, New York: Basic Books, 1983.

Schrank, S. and Ekici, D., eds, *Healing Spaces, Modern Architecture, and the Body*, London: Routledge, 2016.

Sennett, R., *The Craftsman*, New Haven: Yale University Press, 2008.

Serres, M., *The Parasite*, trans. L. R. Schehr, Baltimore: John Hopkins University Press, 1982.

Serres, M., *Genesis*, trans. G. James and J. Nielson, Ann Arbor: University of Michigan Press, 1995.

Setti, L., Passarini, F., De Gennaro, G., Barbieri, P., Perrone, M., Borelli, M., Palmisani, J., Di Gilio, A., Piscitelli, P. and Miani, A., 'Airborne Transmission Route of COVID-19: Why 2 Meters/6 Feet of Inter-Personal Distance Could Not Be Enough', *International Journal of Environmental Research and Public Health*, 17, no. 8 (2020): 2932.

Shapin, S., 'The House of Experiment in Seventeenth-Century England', *Isis*, 79, no. 3 (1988): 373–404.

Shapin, S. and Schaffer, S., *Leviathan and the Air-Pump: Hobbes, Boyle, and the Experimental Life*, Princeton: Princeton University Press, 1985.

Sharif, A., 'Sustainable Architectural Design between Inscription and De-scription: The Case of Masdar City', PhD diss., The University of Manchester, Manchester, 2016.

Shereen, M., Khan, S., Kazmi, A., Bashir, N. and Siddique, R., 'COVID-19 Infection: Origin, Transmission, and Characteristics of Human Coronaviruses', *Journal of Advanced Research*, 24 (2020): 91–8.

Silverberg, D., 'How Covid Turbocharged the QR Revolution', *BBC News*, 22 January 2021. Available online: https://www.bbc.co.uk/news/business-55579480 (accessed 23 August 2021).

Souriau, É., *Les différents modes d'existence, suivi de Du mode d'existence de l'oeuvre à faire*, Paris: Presses Universitaires de France, 2009.

Stenner, P., 'The Risky Truth of Fabulation: Deleuze, Bergson and Durkheim on the Becomings of Religion and Art', *Annual Review of Critical Psychology*, 14 (2018): 169–92.

Sung, J. and Monschauer, Y., 'Changes in Transport Behaviour During The COVID-19 Crisis', *IEA*, 27 May 2020. Available online: https://www.iea.org/articles/changes-in-transport-behaviour-during-the-COVID-19-crisis (accessed 18 January 2021).

Tarde, G., *Monadologie et sociologie*, Paris: Les empêcheurs de penser en rond, 1999a.

Tarde, G., *Les lois sociales: esquisse d'une sociologie*, Paris: Synthélabo-les Empêcheurs de penser en rond, 1999b.

The Lancet Respiratory Medicine, 'COVID-19 Transmission—Up in the Air', *The Lancet Respiratory Medicine*, 8, no. 12 (2020): 1159.

Thrift, N., 'Re-inventing Invention: New Tendencies in Capitalist Commodification', *Economy and Society*, 35, no. 2 (2006): 279–306.

Till, J., *Architecture Depends*, Cambridge, MA: MIT Press, 2009.

Transport Focus, 'Week 34: Journey Satisfaction During COVID-19', *Transport Focus*, 2020. Available online: https://www.transportfocus.org.uk/publication/journey-satisfaction-during-COVID-19-week-34/ (accessed 18 January 2021).

UK Government, 'Working Safely During COVID-19 in Offices and Contact Centres', *COVID-19 Secure Guidance for Employers, Employees and the Self- Employed*, 5 November 2020. Available online: https://assets.publishing.service.gov.uk/media/5eb97e76866 50c278d4496ea/working-safely-during-covid-19-offices-contact-centres-041120.pdf (accessed 5 August 2021).

Walker, S., 'Fairground Architecture and the Crowds', *Architectural Theory Review*, 23, no. 2 (2019): 256–86.

Whittle, N., 'Welcome to the 15-Minute City', *Financial Times*, 17 July 2020. Available online: https://www.ft.com/content/c1a53744-90d5-4560-9e3f-17ce06aba69a (accessed 15 January 2021).

Yaneva, A., 'Scaling up and Down: Extraction Trials in Architectural Design', *Social Studies of Science*, 35 (2005): 867–94.

Yaneva, A., *The Making of a Building: A Pragmatist Approach to Architecture*, Oxford: Peter Lang AG, 2009a.

Yaneva, A., *Made by the Office for Metropolitan Architecture. An Ethnography of Design*, Rotterdam: 010 Publishers, 2009b.

Yaneva, A., *Mapping Controversies in Architecture*, Farnham: Ashgate, 2012.
Yaneva, A., *Five Ways to Make Architecture Political: An Introduction to the Politics of Design Practice*, London: Bloomsbury, 2017.
Yaneva, A., 'New Voices in Architectural Ethnography', *Ardeth (Architectural Design Theory)*, 1, no. 2 (2018): 17–35.
Yaneva, A., *Crafting History: Archiving and the Quest for Architectural Legacy*, Ithaca: Cornell University Press, 2020.
Yaneva, A., 'Choreographies for the Laboratorized City', *Architectural Theory Review*, 24, no. 2 (2020): 188–91.
Yarrow, T., *Architects: Portraits of a Practice*, Ithaca: Cornell University Press, 2019.
Yeung, P., 'How '15-Minute Cities' Will Change The Way We Socialise', *BBC.com*, 2021. Available online: https://www.bbc.com/worklife/article/20201214-how-15-minute-cities-will-change-the-way-we-socialise (accessed 15 August 2021).
Yeung, Y., Chow, W. and Lam, V., 'Sick Building Syndrome – A Case Study', *Building and Environment*, 26, no. 4 (1991): 319–30.

INDEX

aboriginal communities 134
accountability 76, 85, 102, 106
Actor-Network-Theory 13, 83
adjustment, adjustments 4, 14,
 83, 85–6, 103, 108, 121,
 143–6, 149, 154–6
airport, airports 2, 43, 48, 52,
 59, 62–3
anthropologist 15–17, 75, 86
anthropology 17, 154
architectural knowledge 5,
 13–14, 144
architectural theory 14, 155
Argentina 83, 158 n.28
Asana 125, 129
atomization 96, 98, 119
atomized 77, 119
attachments 3, 121
Australia 83, 99, 133–4,
 160 n.64
Austria 83, 96, 158 n.16,
 160 n.3
AutoCAD 114, 118, 124
autonomy 81, 108

background expectancies 84–5,
 131
balance of forces 33–5, 72, 75
balance of power 36
banlieue 141
becoming real 38
BIM 122–5, 129

Brazil 83, 124, 158 n.26,
 158 n.32, 159 n.50
breaching experiment 84–5,
 105–6, 120, 130–1, 145
bubble, bubbles 51–2, 77, 79,
 90, 96–7
Bulgaria 83
bus 42–3, 45, 51, 56

Canada 83, 112, 128, 159 n.52,
 160 n.63
China 29, 83, 96, 123, 126,
 158 n.19, 159 n.44,
 159 n.49, 159 n.53, 160 n.68,
 160 n.74, 161 n.4
civic resilience 139–40
cleaning products 60
client 3–4, 22–3, 85, 90–2, 95,
 99, 106, 111–12, 125–6,
 130–1, 133–4, 136–7,
 141–5, 149, 151, 154
Colomina, Beatriz 11, 22–3, 78
commuter 41–2
contactless 14, 34, 54, 56–7,
 59–61, 66–7, 76, 78–9, 148
contagion 89
container 72, 78, 102
containment 77
counting bodies 44–6, 64, 67
craftsman, craftsmen 90, 119, 146
Cuff, Dana 15, 82, 106, 120,
 158 n.31, 159 n.47

INDEX

Cyprus 83, 112, 128
the Czech Republic 83, 158 n.21

Deleuze, Gilles 2, 34, 38
Denmark 83
diffusion model 28–30
digital
 technologies 57, 79, 121–2, 124, 128
 tools 122–3, 127, 129–31, 144
 turn 116, 121–2, 124
digitally enhanced sketching 121
discovery 28, 150
disinfection 60–1
dispositif, dispositifs 2, 13, 34–6, 38, 48–50, 54, 56, 64, 67, 70–2, 74–5, 78–9, 94, 136, 141, 144, 148–9, 151
disruption, disruptions 85–6, 121, 147
distant
 ethnography 14–17, 82
 reading, readings 7, 9–10, 154–5
domestic spaces 4
droplets 20, 26, 28, 55–6, 64, 79

electronic pen 117, 121
empathy 88–9, 95, 152–3
entrapment 34, 38–9, 74–6, 78, 148
epidemiologists 11, 32, 34
epistemic habits 4, 13, 82, 149
ethnographic
 observation 12, 15, 39, 82, 86
 photography 17
 questionnaire 13–14, 16, 83, 85
ethnomethodology 84
ethnomethods 85
experiment 32, 36, 82, 84–5, 101, 144

fables 38
fabulation 38–9, 75
face
 covering 60, 62, 64, 67–8
 mask 64, 70
false autonomy 81
feedback loop 95–6, 98, 124
flexibility 33, 56, 64, 92, 109
Forty, Adrian 22, 106, 109–10
Foucault, Michel 2, 50, 136
France 83, 90, 160 n.67, 160 n.70

Garfinkel, Harold 84–5, 145
Gell, Alfred 75–6
Germany 83, 157 n.6, 157 n.12, 158 n.16, 160 n.66, 160 n.69, 169 n.3
Greece 83, 153, 158 n.24, 160 n.73, 161 n.6

hand sketching 114–15
health
 agencies 59
 care 22
 checks, checking 59, 67
 code 48
 condition 50
 control 59
 measures 2
 problems 23
 products 59
 QR code 59
hierarchies 101, 103, 106, 112, 120, 130–1, 144, 149
historians of science 11
historicity 150
historiographies 12
history 17, 21, 150–1, 154–5
Hong Kong 23–5, 83, 111, 129, 142, 159 n.37, 160 n.59
host, hosts 20–2, 37–8, 52, 75, 139
hygienists 3, 12, 32, 73–4

illness 22–3, 44, 77, 79, 152
imitation 77, 145
India 83
indoor spaces 25–6
innovation, innovations 13–14, 24, 28, 59–60, 83, 85–6, 115, 125, 144–5, 149, 151
inscription, inscriptions 27–8, 38
instrument, instruments 1, 4, 27–8, 34–5
interruption, interruptions 5, 84–5, 97
invention, inventions 38, 63, 85, 107, 145
Ireland 83, 95–6, 158 n.17
Israel 83, 126, 159 n.54
Italy 14, 83, 87–8, 110, 157 n.1, 157 nn.4–6, 157 nn.8–9, 158 n.20, 158 nn.34–5, 159 n.36, 159 n.39, 160 n.69
IT infrastructure 122
IT tools 122

Jordan 83, 114, 117, 158 n.15, 158 n.25, 159 n.42, 160 n.75

Kosovo 83, 127, 159 n.57

lab-like settings 2, 13, 21, 24, 26, 31–6, 38–9, 56, 71–3, 75–8, 151
laboratorization 2, 12, 32–3, 35–8, 147
Latour, Bruno 3–4, 12, 26–8, 35, 72, 82, 84, 86, 155
library 23–4, 34, 43–4, 46, 56–60, 62, 64, 71
lines of sight 49
Lithuania 83
lockdown 3, 6, 9, 14, 19, 40, 42–3, 59, 81, 83, 87–9, 91, 93, 99, 102, 105, 107, 110, 115, 133–4, 142–3
Loos, Adolf 109, 119–20

making noise 20, 150
Malta 83, 89, 157 n.7
mask, masks 48, 59, 64, 69–70, 74, 76–8, 88–9, 99, 134, 137
matter of fact 34
mental health 10, 68, 86
metamorphosis, metamorphoses 13, 21, 77, 144, 148–9, 151, 155
method 12, 14, 16–17, 25, 102, 106, 117, 124, 128, 131, 133, 136, 142, 152, 154–5
methods of architectural research 14
minimal
 actions 131, 144, 148
 angles 148
 change, changes 13–14, 145
 inclinations 77
modern architecture 22–3, 66
modulor 64, 66, 148
Moretti, Franco 7, 9
museum, museums 21, 37, 43, 52, 57–8

the Netherlands 83
network, networks 2, 7, 9, 12, 28–9, 31–4, 72–4, 139, 146, 150–1, 154
Neurath, Otto 67–8, 109
New Zealand 83, 159 n.46
noise 20–1, 30, 71, 74, 99, 150–1

office
 buildings 48, 50, 52, 60
 space 50, 86, 88, 90, 92, 102, 135
outbreak 19, 24, 29–30, 41, 47

INDEX

pandemic
  city 14, 17, 33, 38, 42, 68, 76, 94
  designers 146
  design practice 13, 146
  designs 36
  formats of practice 156
  health hazard 107
  practice, practices 7, 145, 149
  parasite 19–20, 81, 147
  perfectionism 119–20
  performance, performances 28, 70, 78, 97, 129
  Perspex 39, 54–6, 72, 78, 148
  pictogram, pictograms 13, 34, 36, 50, 54, 56, 65, 67–70, 74, 148, 150
  pictogram language 67
  plexiglas 54
  politicians 3, 12, 27–8, 30–1, 34, 72–3
  Portugal 83
post-pandemic
  city, cities 154, 156
  era 156
power 2–3, 12–13, 21, 27, 33, 36, 38–9, 70, 75–6, 156
pragmatist
  approach 35
  approach to history writing 155
primary design 103, 121
project management 124–8, 131
public health 8, 14, 74
  agencies 59
  experts 12
  professionals 34
  servants 28, 30, 72
  specialists 32
public transport, transportation 37, 40–3, 45, 56, 64, 68

QR code, codes 58–9

reflexivity 5, 11, 81, 114, 121, 136, 152
Republic of North Macedonia 83, 96, 158 n.18, 159 n.41, 160 n.2
responsibilities 110, 112, 139, 149
revolving door 54
Ricoeur, Paul 155
roles 110–12, 118, 124, 130–1, 149
Russia 83, 160 n.72

sanatorium 23
sanitizer 43, 60–2, 72, 78, 148
sanitizing machine 63
Schön, Donald 15, 108
science and technology studies 32
scientists 3, 11–12, 26–30, 32, 34–5, 71–3
Sennett, Richard 119
sequential photography 39
Serbia 83
Serres, Michell 12, 20, 37, 66, 77, 147
shop, shops 5, 33, 43, 45, 56, 58, 60, 68, 106
Sick Building Syndrome (SBS) 22–4
Slovenia 83, 158 n.13
social
  distancing 25, 29, 39, 42–3, 50, 54, 57, 68, 70, 78, 83, 146, 154, 156
  explanation 30, 36
  habits 42
  interaction, interactions 15, 33, 62, 64, 84
  link, links 3, 5, 148
Souriau, Etienne 101

Spain 83, 96, 112–13, 128, 158 n.23, 159 n.38, 159 n.40, 159 n.56, 160 n.1
spatial
architecture 24, 77–9, 81, 147
arrangement, arrangements 5, 13, 30, 38, 93, 144
choreography 2, 26, 39, 41, 44, 71, 94, 147
conventions 3, 14, 39, 67, 71, 77
organization 43, 77
practice, practices 13, 38, 42–3, 67, 70
routines 4, 13
spokespersons 27, 36, 72
store 44–5, 56, 59, 62, 70
storytelling 106–7, 124, 144
surrogate 134–6, 141, 144, 151
Sweden 83
Switzerland 83, 142

tactics 4, 14–15, 34, 50, 85, 98, 136, 141, 144, 147, 154
technology 44, 47–50, 78, 121–2, 125–6, 128, 132, 148
tele-working 142
temperature
check, checks 47, 59, 68
devices 50
door 48
kiosks 48
measuring gun 47, 49
measuring infrared camera 49, 76
measuring robots 48, 72, 78, 148
measuring technologies 47
theatre of proof 35, 37, 72
theatre of truth 35
thick description 14, 156

Till, Jeremy 38, 81, 141
togetherness 38, 71, 89–90, 92, 94, 99, 100, 117
train, trains 42–4, 51, 56, 71
train station, stations 2, 43–4, 50, 57, 59, 62
translation model 30
trap, traps 20, 34, 39, 75–6, 78
tuberculosis 22–3
Turkey 83

the United Kingdom 83
the United States 23, 83, 92
urban
dwellers 2, 6, 11, 13, 31, 39, 42, 50, 66–7, 70–2
life 2–3, 10–11, 13–14, 17, 21, 33, 38–9, 41–2, 61, 67, 71, 74, 76, 79

variants 12, 19, 29–32
Venezuela 83, 88, 91, 157 n.3, 157 n.10
ventilation 20, 22–4, 55, 60, 64, 68, 92–3
verbal expression 104, 119
virologists 11–12
visibility 2, 34, 49, 56, 64, 77–9, 94, 148

Wacom 114–15, 119, 142
well-being 67, 86, 92, 129
Whitehead, Alfred North 150
Wittgenstein, Ludwig 119–20
working
habits 3, 81, 93, 121, 144
patterns 14
space, spaces 4, 92–3
workload 98, 129
World Health Organization (WHO) 19, 25
written expression 106, 109, 120